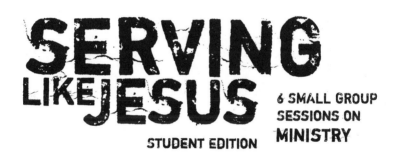

SERVING
LIKE JESUS

6 SMALL GROUP
SESSIONS ON
MINISTRY

STUDENT EDITION

DOUG FIELDS &
BRETT EASTMAN

II1016315

ZONDERVAN™

GRAND RAPIDS, MICHIGAN 49530 USA

ZONDERVAN.COM/
AUTHORTRACKER

Youth Specialties

www.youthspecialties.com

Youth Specialties

Serving in Jesus, Student Edition: Six Sessions on Ministry
Copyright © 2006 by Doug Fields and Brett Eastman

Youth Specialties products, 300 South Pierce Street, El Cajon, CA 92020,
are published by Zondervan, 5300 Patterson Avenue SE, Grand Rapids,
MI 49530

Library of Congress Cataloging-in-Publication Data

Fields, Doug, 1962-
  Serving like Jesus : 6 small group sessions on ministry / Doug Fields and
Brett Eastman.
      p. cm. -- (Experiencing Christ together, student edition)
  ISBN-10: 0-310-26647-5 (pbk.)
  ISBN-13: 978-0-310-26647-1 (pbk.)
  1. Church work--Biblical teaching. 2. Lay ministry--Biblical teaching.
3. Service (Theology)--Biblical teaching. 4. Church work--Study and
teaching. 5. Lay ministry--Study and teaching. 6. Service (Theology)--
Study and teaching. I. Eastman, Brett, 1959- II. Title.

BV4400.F54 2006
268'.433--dc22

                                                            2005024175

Creative Team: Dave Urbanski, Holly Sharp, Mark Novelli, Joanne Heim,
Janie Wilkerson
Cover Design: Mattson Creative
Printed in the United States of America

06 07 08 09 10 • 10 9 8 7 6 5 4 3 2

ACKNOWLEDGMENTS

This series of six books couldn't have happened if there weren't some wonderful friends who chimed in on the process and added their heart and level of expertise to these pages. I need to acknowledge and thank my friends for loving God, caring for students and supporting me-especially true on this task were Amanda Maguire, Nancy Varner, Ryanne Dearden, Jana Sarti, Matt McGill and the crew at Simply Youth Ministry. I sure appreciate doing life together. Also, I'm very appreciative of Brett Eastman for asking me to do this project.

TABLE OF CONTENTS

INTRODUCTION: READ ME FIRST!

Welcome to a Journey with Jesus (and Others)!

I hope you're ready for God to do something great in your life as you use this book and connect with a few friends and a loving small group leader. The potential of this combination is incredible. The reason we know its potential is because we've heard from thousands of students who've already gone through our first series of LIFETOGETHER books and shared their stories. We've been blessed to hear that the combination of friends gathering together, books with great questions, and the Bible as a foundation have provided the ingredients for life change. As you read these words, know that you're beginning a journey that may revolutionize your life.

The following six sessions are designed to help you grow in your knowledge of Jesus and his teachings and become his devoted disciple. But growth doesn't happen alone. You need God's help and a community of people who love God, too. We've found that a great way to grow strong in Christ is in the context of a caring, spiritual community (or small group). This community is committed to doing life together—at least for a season—and will thrive when each small group member (you) focuses on Jesus as well as the others in the group.

This type of spiritual community isn't easy. It requires several things from you:

- trust
- confidentiality
- honesty
- care
- openness
- risk
- commitment to meet regularly

Anyone can meet with a few people and call it a "group," but it takes stronger commitment and desire to create a spiritual community where others can know you, love you, care for you, and give you the freedom to open up about your thoughts, doubts, and struggles—a place where you're safe to be yourself.

We've learned from the small groups that didn't work that spiritual community can't develop without honesty. Now, at first you may be tempted to show up to your small group session and sit, smile, act nicely, and never speak from your heart—but this type of superficial participation prevents true spiritual community. Please fight through this temptation and know that when you reveal who you really are, you'll contribute something unique and powerful to the group that can't occur any other way. Your honest sharing about your heart and soul will challenge other group members to do the same, and they'll likely become as honest as you are.

To help you get to this place of honesty, every session contains questions that are intended to push you to think, talk, and open your heart. They'll challenge you to expose some of your fears, hurts, and habits. Through them, I guarantee you'll experience spiritual growth and relational intimacy, and you'll build lasting, genuine friendships.

All mature Christians will tell you that God used others to impact their lives. God has a way of allowing one life to connect with another to result in richer, deeper, and more vibrant lives for both. As you go through this book (and the five others in this series), you will have the opportunity to impact someone else—and someone else will have the opportunity to impact you. You'll both become deeper, stronger followers of Jesus Christ. So get ready for some life change.

WHO IS JESUS?

Most people have an opinion about Jesus. But many of these opinions are based on what they've heard or come up with on their own—what they'd *prefer* Jesus to be—as opposed to their own discovery of Jesus through the Bible. People believe Jesus was all kinds of things—a great teacher, a leader of a revolution, a radical with a political agenda, a gentle man with a big vision, a prophet, a spiritual person who emphasized religion. Still others believe he is who he claimed to be—God.

The Jesus of the Bible is far more compelling than most people's opinions about him. *Serving Like Jesus* allows you to get to know Jesus as his first followers did. They met Jesus as Teacher, a rabbi. They came to know Jesus as Healer, Shepherd, Servant, Savior, and ultimately the One who defeated death—the risen Lord. From his first words, "Follow me," through his ministry, death, and resurrection, he kept drawing people deeper into his life.

Jesus asked his disciples to commit their lives to God's way. As you read the Bible, you'll see that God's ways weren't always easy or comfortable for the disciples to follow. But what motivated them to do what he taught was their rich experience of who he was and all he did for them. *Serving Like Jesus* will ground you in that same experience so you'll more fully desire to follow Jesus and commit to his ways—even when it's not easy or comfortable. The Jesus you're about to encounter is waiting for you to meet him, get closer to him, and commit your life to following his ways and teachings.

When you align your life with Jesus, you're in for a wild, adventurous life. It won't be without its difficulties, but it'll be a better life than you ever dreamed possible.

WHAT YOU NEED TO KNOW ABOUT EACH OF THESE SIX SESSIONS

Each session in this study contains more material than you and your group can complete in a typical meeting of an hour or so. The key to making the most of each session is to choose which questions you'll answer and discuss and which ones you'll save for your alone time. We've tried to make it simple, so if you miss something from one meeting, you can pick it up the next time you're together. Let's be more specific.

Each of the six sessions in *Serving Like Jesus* contains five unique sections. These five sections have the same titles in every book and in every session in the LIFETOGETHER series. The sections are (1) fellowship, (2) discipleship, (3) ministry, (4) evangelism, and (5) worship. These represent five biblical purposes that we believe lead to personal spiritual growth, growth in your student ministry, and health for your entire church. The more you think about these five purposes and try to make them part of your life, the stronger you'll be and the more you'll grow spiritually.

While these five biblical purposes make sense individually, they can make a greater impact when they're brought together. Think of it in sports terms: If you play baseball or softball, you might be an outstanding hitter—but you also need to catch, throw, run, and slide. You need more than one skill to impact your team. In the same way, having a handle on one or two of the five biblical purposes is great—but when they're all reflected together in a person's life, that person is much more biblically balanced and healthy.

You'll find that the material in this book (and in the other LIFETOGETHER books) is built around the Bible. There are a lot of blank spaces and journaling pages where you can write down your thoughts about God's Word and God's work in your life as you explore and live out God's biblical purposes.

Each session begins with a short story that helps introduce the theme. If you have time to read it, great—if not, no big deal. Immediately following the story are five key sections. The following is a brief description of each:

♥ FELLOWSHIP: CONNECTING YOUR HEART TO OTHERS

Goal: To share about your life and listen attentively to others, caring about what they share

You'll begin your session with a few minutes of conversation that will give you all a chance to share from your own lives, get to know each other better, and offer initial thoughts about the session's theme. The icon for this section is a heart because you're opening up your heart so others can connect with you on a deeper level.

DISCIPLESHIP: GROWING TO BE LIKE JESUS

Goal: To explore God's Word, gain biblical knowledge, and make personal applications

This section will take the most time. You'll explore the Bible and gain some knowledge about Jesus. You'll encounter his life and teachings and discuss how God's Word can make a difference in your own life. The icon for this section is a brain because you're opening your mind to learn God's Word and his ways.

You'll find lots of questions in this section—more than you can discuss during your group time. Your leader will choose the questions you have time to discuss or come up with different questions. We encourage you to respond to the skipped questions on your own; during the week it's a great way to get more Bible study time.

MINISTRY: SERVING OTHERS IN LOVE

Goal: To recognize and take advantage of opportunities to serve others

When you get to this section, you'll have an opportunity to discuss how to express God's love through serving others. The discussion and opportunities are created to tie into the topic. As you grow spiritually, you'll naturally begin to recognize and take opportunities to serve others. As your heart grows, so will your opportunities to serve. Here, the icon is a foot because feet communicate movement and action—serving and meeting the needs of others requires you to act on what you've learned.

✏ EVANGELISM: SHARING YOUR STORY AND GOD'S STORY

Goal: To consider how the truths from this session might be applied to your relationships with unbelievers

It's very easy for a small group to turn into a clique that only looks inward and loses sight of others outside the group. That's not God's plan. God wants you to reach out to people with his message of love and life change. While this is often scary, this section will give you an opportunity to discuss your relationships with non-Christians and consider ways to listen to their stories, share pieces of your story, and reflect the amazing love of God's story. The icon for this section is a mouth because you're opening your mouth to have spiritual conversations with nonbelievers.

✗ WORSHIP: SURRENDERING YOUR LIFE TO HONOR GOD

Goal: To focus on God's presence

Each session ends with a time of prayer. You'll be challenged to slow down and turn your focus toward God's love, his goodness, and his presence in your life. You'll spend time talking to God, listening in silence, reading Scripture, writing, and focusing on God. The key word for this time is *surrender*, which is giving up what you want so God can give you what he wants. The icon for this section is a body, which represents surrendering your entire life to God.

Oh yeah…there are more sections in each session!

In addition to the main material, there are several additional options you can use to help further and deepen your times with God. Many people attend church programs, listen, and then "leave" God until the next week when they return to church. We don't want that to happen to you! So we've provided several more opportunities for you to learn, reflect, and grow on your own.

At the end of every session you'll find three more key headings:

- At Home This Week
- Learn a Little More
- For Deeper Study on Your Own

They're fairly easy to figure out, but here's a brief description of each:

AT HOME THIS WEEK

There are five options presented at the end of each session that you can do on your own. They're not homework for the next session (unless your leader assigns them to your group); they're things you can do to keep growing at your own pace. You can skip them, you can do all of them, or you can vary the options from session to session.

Option 1: A Weekly Reflection

At the end of each session you'll find a one-page, quick self-evaluation that helps you reflect on the five key areas of your spiritual life (fellowship, discipleship, ministry, evangelism, and worship). It's simply a guide for you to gauge your spiritual health. The first one is on page 28.

Option 2: Daily Bible Readings

One of the challenges in deepening your knowledge of God's Word and learning more about Jesus' life is to read the Bible on your own. This option provides a guide to help you read through the Gospel of Matthew in 30 days. On pages 109-110 is a list of Bible passages to help you continue to take God's Word deeper into your life.

Option 3: Memory Verses

On pages 114-115 you'll find six Bible verses to memorize. Each is related to the theme of a particular session. (Again, these are optional...remember, nothing is mandatory!)

Option 4: Journaling

You'll find a question or two related to the theme of the session that can serve as a trigger to get you writing. Journaling is a great way to reflect on what you've been learning and evaluate your life. In addition to questions at the end of each session, there's a helpful tool on page 116 that can guide you through the discipline of journaling.

Option 5: Wrap It Up

As you've already read, each session contains too many questions for one small group meeting. So this section provides opportunities to think through your answers to the questions you skipped and then go back and write them down.

LEARN A LITTLE MORE

We've provided some insights (or commentary) on some of the passages that you'll study to help you understand the difficult terms, phrases, and people that you'll read about in each Bible passage.

FOR DEEPER STUDY ON YOUR OWN

One of the best ways to understand the Bible passages and the theme of each session is to dig a little deeper. If deeper study fits your personality style, please use these additional ideas as ways to enhance your learning.

WHAT YOU NEED TO KNOW ABOUT BEING IN A SMALL GROUP

You probably have enough casual or superficial friendships and don't need to waste your time cultivating more. We all need deep and committed friendships. Here are a few ideas to help you benefit the most from your small group time and build great relationships.

Prepare to Participate

Interaction is a key to a good small group. Talking too little will make it hard for others to get to know you. Everyone has something to contribute—yes, even you! But participating doesn't mean dominating, so be careful to not monopolize the conversation. Most groups typically have one conversation hog, and if you don't know who it is in your small group, then it might be you. Here's a tip: You don't have to answer every question and comment on every point. Try to find a balance between the two extremes.

Be Consistent

Healthy relationships take time to grow. Quality time is great, but a great quantity of time is probably better. Commit with your group to show up every week (or whenever your group plans to meet), even when you don't feel like it. With only six sessions per book, if you miss just two meetings you'll have missed a third of what's presented in these pages. When you make a commitment to your small group a high priority, you're sure to build meaningful relationships.

Practice Honesty and Confidentiality

Strong relationships are only as solid as the trust they are built upon. Although it may be difficult, take a risk and be honest with your answers. God wants you to be known by others! Then respect the risks others are taking and offer them the same love, grace, and forgiveness God does. Make confidentiality a nonnegotiable value for your small group. Nothing kills community like gossip.

Arrive Ready to Grow

You can always arrive prepared by praying ahead of time. Ask God to give you the courage to be honest and the discipline to respect others.

You aren't required to do any preparation in the book before you arrive (unless you're the leader—see page 82). If your leader chooses to, she may ask you to do the Disciple-

Doug Fields & Brett Eastman

Doug and Brett were part of the same small group for several years. Brett was the pastor of small groups at Saddleback Church where Doug is the pastor to students. Brett and a team of friends wrote DOING LIFETOGETHER, a group study for adults. Everyone loved it so much that they asked Doug to take the same theme and Bible verses and revise the other material for students. So even though Brett and Doug both had a hand in writing this book, the book you're using is written by Doug—and as a youth pastor, he's cheering you on in your small group experience. For more information on Doug and Brett see page 137.

ship (GROWING) section ahead of time so that you'll have more time to discuss the other sections and make better use of your time.

Congratulations...

...for making a commitment to go through this material with your small group! Life change is within reach when people are united through the same commitment. Your participation in a small group can have a lasting and powerful impact on your life. Our prayer is that the questions and activities in this book help you grow closer to the other group members, and more importantly, to God.

If you're a small group leader, please turn to page 82 for a brief instruction on how best to use this material.

SMALL GROUP COVENANT

One of the signs of a healthy small group is that all members understand its purpose. We've learned that members of good small groups make a bond, a commitment, or a covenant to one another.

Read through the following covenant as a group. Be sure to discuss your concerns and questions before you begin your first session. Please feel free to modify the covenant based on the needs and concerns of your particular group. Once you agree with the terms and are willing to commit to the covenant (as you've revised it), sign your own book and have the others sign yours.

With a covenant, your entire group will have the same purpose for your time together, allowing you to grow together and go deeper into your study of God's Word. Without a covenant, groups often find themselves meeting simply for the sake of meeting.

If your group decides to add some additional values, write them at the bottom of the covenant page. Your group may also want to create some rules (such as not interrupting when someone else is speaking or sitting up instead of lying down). You can list those at the bottom of the covenant page also.

Reviewing your group's covenant, values, and rules before each meeting can become a significant part of your small group experience.

> A covenant is a binding agreement or contract. God made covenants with Noah, Abraham, and David, among others. Jesus is the fulfillment of a new covenant between God and his people.

SMALL GROUP COVENANT

I, _____, as a member of our small group, acknowledge my need for meaningful relationships with other believers. I agree that this small group community exists to help me deepen my relationships with God, Christians, and other people in my life. I commit to the following:

Consistency

I will give my best effort to attend each of our group meetings.

Honesty

I will take risks to share truthfully about the personal issues in my life.

Confidentiality

I will support the foundation of trust in our small group by not participating in gossip. I will not reveal personal information shared by others during our meetings.

Respect

I will help create a safe environment for our small group members by listening carefully and not making fun of others.

Prayer

I commit to pray regularly for the people in our small group.

Accountability

I will allow the people in my small group to hold me accountable for growing spiritually and living a life that honors God.

This covenant, signed by all the members in this group, reflects our commitment to one another.

Date:

Names:

Additional values our small group members agree to

Additional rules our small group members agree to

SERVE YOUR WAY TO SUCCESS

 LEADERS, READ PAGE 82.

Candice noticed that her youth pastor and his wife hung around the sanctuary for a long time after church every Sunday. They stayed to make sure they had plenty of time to talk to students and to clean the youth room. When Candice asked them what time they finally got home after church, she was surprised at the answer: After 5 p.m.!

Candice was floored—youth group ended at noon. She knew they stayed longer because they loved her and her fellow students, but she thought others should share some of the burden to clean up so her youth pastor and family could get home earlier.

She came up with the idea of recruiting a team of students to help clean the youth room while others were hanging out and talking. But Candice found her leadership task a difficult one. Most of the students had great excuses, saying there were other things they needed to do. So Candice cleaned the youth room by herself for the first month—until two other girls volunteered to help out. For a few months the three of them cleaned and organized the room. The thankful response from the youth pastor and his family kept them encouraged. After several months of consistent cleaning, a few more students began to participate in this new clean-up ministry. Candice was thrilled that others finally saw the need and responded by jumping in and serving. Now everyone gets home a lot earlier.

Serving is often anything but glamorous. No one loves picking up trash, stacking chairs, or putting things away. It's easy to view service jobs as beneath us—but they're not. In this session you'll see that no act of service is beneath you if you've acquired the servant heart of Jesus.

♥ FELLOWSHIP: CONNECTING YOUR HEART TO OTHERS

Just a reminder: There probably isn't enough time in your small-group session to answer every question. Instead choose which ones you'll answer, and then answer the others on your own time. Have fun!

Goal: To share about your life and listen attentively to others, caring about what they share

If you're new to this series of books, you'll find that every time you get to the fellowship section, the questions are designed to get you talking and knowing each other better. If you're a veteran of the series (which means that you've been through some of the other books), then you already know what to do.

1. Do you know someone who is considered successful in the eyes of the world? What makes this person successful?

2. What is it about serving that makes it so difficult sometimes?

● DISCIPLESHIP: GROWING TO BE LIKE JESUS

Goal: To explore God's Word, gain biblical knowledge, and make personal applications

No one wakes up in the morning saying, "I hope my life amounts to nothing and that I never make any kind of significant impact." Everyone is wired with some desire to succeed at something. But while our world tells us to be "number one," it also says that we have to look out for "number one" to get there. Many follow this path, but it doesn't deliver fulfillment.

You're about to read a shocking and powerful teaching from Jesus. With just a few words, Jesus turns everything upside down, challenging everything we instinctively believe to be true about success and greatness.

Read Mark 10:36-45. (If you don't have a Bible, the passage is on page 87.)

1. Why do you think James and John ask Jesus their question in verse 36? What do you think prompted them?

2. Why didn't Jesus grant their request?

3. Why do you think the other disciples were bothered ("became indignant") by their desire for greatness?

4. What do you think was wrong with James and John—their desire for greatness or their understanding of what true greatness is? Explain your position and use the Bible passage to support your answer.

5. Respond to this statement: "The drive for greatness isn't as important as one's definition of greatness."

If your group hasn't discussed the small group covenant on page 18, please take some time now to go through it. Make commitments to each other that your group time will reflect those values (and any additional ones you add). One sign of a healthy small group is that it begins each session by reading the covenant together as a constant reminder of what the group has committed to.

6. This passage begins with a bold statement from James and John and may be something of a shock to read. Do you ever feel like you take this attitude with your prayer life—that is, do you boldly ask God for what you want or need? This may be a tough question to answer, but be honest.

7. Did Jesus ridicule James and John for making such a request? Why do you think God says "no" to some of our prayer requests?

8. Why isn't servanthood attractive in our world? In the church?

9. Why do you think Jesus teaches that servanthood is the true path to success?

10. Read verse 45 again. What does it tell you about Jesus' character?

MINISTRY: SERVING OTHERS IN LOVE

Goal: To recognize and take advantage of opportunities to serve others

In the previous passage, Jesus emphasized both humility and sacrifice. *Humility* doesn't mean thinking badly of yourself; it simply means you put others first and don't think of yourself more highly than you should. *Sacrifice*, on the other hand, is something you do for others—and there's always a cost attached. Humility and sacrifice may be hard for you right now, but they become more natural as you learn to see life through Jesus' eyes and start putting them into practice.

1. How do you usually treat people who serve you? (Think about restaurant workers, store clerks, family members, janitors, and so on.)

2. Give examples of how you might "lord it over them" (Mark 10:42).

EVANGELISM: SHARING YOUR STORY AND GOD'S STORY

Goal: To consider how the truths from this session might be applied to your relationships with unbelievers

1. Discuss the following story. How can acts of service become acts of evangelism?

   The Fourth of July in one California beach city meant hundreds of celebrating visitors. By the next morning, trash always littered the streets. Evan decided that it would be great for his youth group to serve the town by picking up the trash. Soon other groups within his church learned about his idea and decided to join in. On the fifth of July, almost 100 people were on the beach and wandering through town, picking up and bagging garbage. They had a great day serving together. It wasn't a glorious task, but the community had a big need and God's servants responded.

   From that day on the city knew Evan's church really cared, and before long, people in the town began asking Evan's church to meet a variety of needs and even to host special events. All this was possible because when there was a need, people responded.

2. Is there an act of service you're doing these days that's also an act of evangelism? If not, what can you do this week that might work for both purposes (service and evangelism)?

For the health of your small group, be sure to read the clique section on pages 98-99.

It's vital for your group to decide at this first session whether you can invite friends to join your group. Talk about the structure of your group and stick to your decision. If you decide the answer is no, you may be able to invite friends to join you in the next EXPERIENCING CHRIST TOGETHER book—there are six of them, so there's plenty of time! If you're a small-group leader, see the Small Group Leader Checklist on page 82.

WORSHIP: SURRENDERING YOUR LIFE TO HONOR GOD

Goal: To focus on God's presence

You'll find three prayer resources in the appendices in the back of this book. By reading them (and possibly discussing them), you'll find your group prayer time more rewarding.
• Praying in Your Small Group (pages 125-126). Read this article on your own before the next session.
• Prayer Request Guidelines (pages 127-128). Read and discuss these guidelines as a group.
• Prayer Options (pages 129-130). Refer to this list for ideas to add variety to your prayer time.

1. Read the following instructions first, and then assign reading parts.

    - Read Philippians 2:6-11 (on pages 87-88) aloud as a group.
    - Next, have one person read the passage slowly while the rest of the group members close their eyes and focus on the words.
    - After the passage is read, have another person read this question: *What does it mean for you to consider others better than yourself?* Sit with that question for a minute and consider your answer.
    - After one minute, have someone read this question (eyes still closed): *How could your life be different if you lived by this section of Scripture?*

2. If you have time, discuss your answers to the two questions. If you don't have time, close the group in prayer.

AT HOME THIS WEEK

One of the consistent values of our LIFETOGETHER books is that we want you to have options for growing spiritually on your own during the week. To help with this "on your own" value, we'll give you five options. If you do these, you'll have more to contribute when you return to your small group, and you'll begin to develop spiritual habits that can last your entire life. Here are the five you'll see after every section. (You might try to do one per day on the days after your small group meets.)

Option 1: A Weekly Reflection

After each session you'll find a quick, one-page self-evalua-tion that reflects the five areas of your spiritual life found in this book (fellowship, discipleship, ministry, evangelism, and worship). After each evaluation, you decide if there's anything you'll do differently with your life. This page is all for you. It's not intended as a report card that you turn into your small group leader. The first evaluation is on page 28.

Option 2: Daily Bible Readings

On pages 109-110 you'll find a list of Bible passages that will help you read through an entire section of the Bible in 30 days. If you choose this option, try to read one of the assigned pas-sages each day. Highlight key verses in your Bible, reflect on them, journal about them, or write down any questions you have from your reading. We want to encourage you to take time to read God's love letter—the Bible. You'll find helpful tips in "How to Study the Bible on Your Own" (page 111).

Option 3: Memory Verses

Memorizing Bible verses is an important habit to develop as you learn to grow spiritually on your own. "Memory Verses" (pages 114-115) contains six verses for you to memorize—one per session. Memorizing verses (and making them stick for more than a few minutes) isn't easy, but the benefits are unde-niable. You'll have God's Word with you wherever you go.

> "I HAVE HIDDEN YOUR WORD IN MY HEART THAT I MIGHT NOT SIN AGAINST YOU. (PSALM 119:11)

Option 4: Journaling

You'll find blank pages for journaling beginning on page 119. At the end of each session, you'll find questions to get your thoughts going—but you aren't limited to answering the questions listed. Use these pages to reflect, write a letter to God, note what you're learning, compose prayer, ask ques-tions, draw pictures, record your thoughts, or take notes if your small group is using the EXPERIENCING CHRIST TOGETHER DVD teachings. For some suggestions about journaling, turn to "Journaling: Snapshots of Your Heart" on page 116.

For this session, choose one or more questions to kickstart your journaling.

Of the five options listed here, mark the option(s) that seem most appealing to you. Share with your group the one(s) you plan to do in the upcoming week. This helps you keep one another accountable as you continue to study and grow on your own.

- I'm excited to be in a group because...
- If someone asked me to describe Jesus, I would say...
- Jesus would want me to know...

Option 5: Wrap It Up

Write out your answers to any questions that you didn't answer during your small group time.

LEARN A LITTLE MORE

Goal: To help you better understand the Scripture passage you studied in this session by highlighting key words and other important information.

James and John (Mark 10:35)

James and John were brothers who worked in their father's fishing business until Jesus called them to become disciples (Mark 1:19-20). They were nicknamed "Sons of Thunder" (3:17), probably a reference to their father's temperament.

Glory (10:37)

The glory of God is his majesty—the outpouring of his presence. We are too fragile and finite to take in God's complete, full presence. (Imagine standing on the surface of the sun—you wouldn't last long!) Instead we experience his glory (see Exodus 33:18-20). Ezekiel 39:21 says, "I will display my glory among the nations, and all the nations will see the punishment I inflict and the hand I lay upon them." Jesus was the glory of God here on earth. In this passage, James and John are talking about the future, the time when Jesus will come in his full presence and glory.

The cup I drink (10:38)

The cup Jesus was to drink was God's judgment on the sins of the world. When Jesus took these sins upon himself on the cross, he left himself open to the judgment God would otherwise unleash upon us. (Also see Mark 14:36.)

To sit at my right or left is not for me to grant (10:40)

Sitting at the right or left of a king was considered a great honor. Jesus already promised the disciples that they would sit on thrones, judging the 12 tribes of Israel (Matthew 19:28). But James and John were looking for even greater honor. Jesus was the Son of God, but he lived in obedience to the direction of God the Father. These positions were not for Jesus to assign. While it is natural to ask, "Who will sit there?" Scripture is silent on this issue.

Slave (10:44)

In the original language of the New Testament (Greek), the word for slave is *doulos*. Paul called himself Christ's *doulos*— Jesus' slave (Romans 1:1). We don't own ourselves; our Master (Jesus) bought us with his blood (1 Corinthians 6:19-20). Here Jesus urges us not only to consider ourselves his slaves, but also slaves to one another! Jesus uses this graphic word to impress on us an attitude of selfless service to the world around us.

Ransom (10:45)

The Greek word for ransom (*lytron*) literally means the price of one's release. Jesus' own life is payment—a ransom—for our release from slavery in sin, allowing us to spend eternity with God.

FOR DEEPER STUDY ON YOUR OWN

1. Check out Philippians 2:1-14 for a picture of humility and servanthood. What are some qualities mentioned in this passage that you'd like to add to your life?

2. Why do you think humility is so important to God? (See Luke 14:11 and James 4:6 for some help.)

3. Why did Jesus oppose the human tendency to put spiritual leaders on pedestals (Matthew 23:1-12)?

A WEEKLY REFLECTION

Take a minute to reflect on how well you've been doing in the following five areas of your spiritual life this week—a 10 means you did an amazing job. This reflection can serve as a spiritual gauge to help you consider some very important areas. This is for your personal evaluation and growth; it's NOT a test—no one else needs to see it.

FELLOWSHIP: CONNECTING YOUR HEART TO OTHERS
How well did I connect with other Christians?

1   2   3   4   5   6   7   8   9   10

DISCIPLESHIP: GROWING TO BE LIKE JESUS
How well did I take steps to grow spiritually and deepen my faith on my own?

1   2   3   4   5   6   7   8   9   10

MINISTRY: SERVING OTHERS IN LOVE

How well did I recognize opportunities to serve others and follow through?

1   2   3   4   5   6   7   8   9   10

EVANGELISM: SHARING YOUR STORY AND GOD'S STORY

How well did I engage in spiritual conversations with non-Christians?

1   2   3   4   5   6   7   8   9   10

WORSHIP: SURRENDERING YOUR LIFE TO HONOR GOD

How well did I focus on God's presence and honor him with my life? Was my relationship with God a primary focus?

1   2   3   4   5   6   7   8   9   10

When you finish, celebrate the areas where you feel good and consider how you can use those strengths to help others in their journey to be more like Jesus. You might also want to take time to identify some potential areas for growth.

SERVING JESUS WHILE SERVING OTHERS

 LEADERS, READ PAGE 82.

Kevin and his family went to Romania with a mission team. The mission's goal was to visit churches, help with repairs, and encourage Christian leaders in Romania. While on the mission, they learned of a nearby orphanage also in need of repairs. While the orphanage wasn't on their agenda, Kevin and his dad decided they could easily do the repairs without the others.

When they reached the orphanage, Kevin was shocked by the number of children living in such a small building. He saw many boys his age who had lived there for more than 10 years. He talked to one boy named Nicolae who knew only a little bit of English. He told Kevin that the children usually got one meal a day and that each child had only one set of clothes. Their clothes had to be worn for several days before being washed.

Kevin's heart ached. He had to do something to serve these boys. As the week came to an end, Kevin looked at all the clothes he'd brought on the trip, thought of Nicolae and the other boys, and decided to drop off his luggage at the orphanage. This prompted others from the trip to do the same. Kevin returned home with only the clothes he was wearing and incredible joy in his heart.

Kevin displayed one aspect of a servant's heart. That's what this session is about—learning to serve someone in need just as if you were serving Jesus himself.

♥ FELLOWSHIP: CONNECTING YOUR HEART TO OTHERS

Goal: To share about your life and listen attentively to others, caring about what they share

What's your strongest memory of someone reaching out to you and serving you when you were in need? If you can't think of an instance, what about when someone did this for your parents? Your family? A family friend?

DISCIPLESHIP: GROWING TO BE LIKE JESUS

Goal: To explore God's Word, gain biblical knowledge, and make personal applications

One of humanity's biggest problems is selfishness. From an early age we're taught to look after our own needs. And selfishness isn't just a problem for unbelievers—it's a significant issue with Christians, too. It's all too easy to fall back into old patterns of serving ourselves. The passage you're about to study is a challenge that Jesus gave his followers 2,000 years ago that's still relevant today.

Read Matthew 25:31-46. (If you don't have a Bible, the passage is on pages 88-89.)

1. Why do you think Jesus will separate everyone into two groups? Is this fair? Explain why you think the way you do.

2. Within the first four verses, three different names (or descriptions) are given to Jesus. What are they, and what is significant about each one?

3. This passage gives us a snapshot of the future. How does a peek at what's coming help you today?

4. What's the difference between the sheep and the goats? What are the consequences of the sheep's actions? The goats' actions?

5. What are the six needs listed in this passage? What do they have in common?

6. In your world, who are the "least of these"? Be specific as you answer this question.

7. In verses 37-39, the righteous ask the king a question, as if they are unsure about why they've been chosen. Why do you think they ask this question? Wouldn't they know the good that they'd done?

8. Does this passage mean that everyone who does good things will experience salvation? Explain your answer.

9. Based on what you know about the Bible, what is the connection between faith and works (serving others)?

10. How is this passage challenging to you? Be specific and come up with at least one challenge.

MINISTRY: SERVING OTHERS IN LOVE

Goal: To recognize and take advantage of opportunities to serve others

It can be difficult to go out on our own to feed the hungry, care for strangers, visit people in prison, and so on. Part of being in community means we can serve together as well as encourage each other in the serving we do on our own.

1. Discuss a service-oriented project your group could undertake together before you finish this book. Do something together that serves the needs of an individual or a group outside your own group. Feeding the hungry, providing water for the thirsty, inviting strangers to your home, clothing the poor, caring for the sick, or visiting prisoners—all these are good ideas. Chances are very good that there are already service organizations within your community doing these things—and you can simply join them if you have difficulty coming up with an idea on your own.

Make sure your group leader doesn't carry all the responsibility to make this service project happen. Work together to get it done!

2. What about serving on your own? Do you know an elderly couple that needs help with tasks around their home? How could you serve a single mother in your church? Make a list of some ideas that you might be able to do in your own neighborhood. Share those ideas.

EVANGELISM: SHARING YOUR STORY AND GOD'S STORY

Goal: To consider how the truths from this session might be applied to your relationships with unbelievers

1. Below is a list of the six actions from the passage you just studied. Take a little time and evaluate which ministry opportunity you think is most difficult and which is easiest. Then give your opinion on which action is the best way to share about Jesus (number them 1 through 6).

Action	Ministry difficulty (1 is most difficult)	Evangelism opportunity (1 is best opportunity)
I was hungry		
I was thirsty		
I was a stranger		
I needed clothes		
I was sick		
I was in prison		

2. There's a fine line between evangelism and ministry—one often leads to the other. Have you learned anything new from numbering the previous list? If so, what is it? (By the way, there is no one correct way to list 1 through 6!)

🚶 WORSHIP: SURRENDERING YOUR LIFE TO HONOR GOD

Goal: To focus on God's presence

1. Share your biggest hurdle to becoming a more servant-hearted person. Turn these answers into prayer requests and pray for each other.

2. Read these words over several times (aloud or silently) and picture what that scene might look like. Hang on to that mental picture as you close your time in prayer.

"WHEN THE SON OF MAN COMES IN HIS GLORY, AND ALL THE ANGELS WITH HIM, HE WILL SIT ON HIS THRONE IN HEAVENLY GLORY." (MATTHEW 25:31)

AT HOME THIS WEEK

Option 1: A Weekly Reflection

Take another self-evaluation that reflects five areas of your spiritual life (fellowship, discipleship, ministry, evangelism, and worship). See page 38.

Option 2: Daily Bible Readings

Check out the Bible reading plan on pages 109-110.

Option 3: Memory Verses

Memorize another verse from pages 114-115.

Option 4: Journaling

Choose one or more of the following options:

- Write down whatever is on your mind.
- Read your journal entry from last week and write a reflection about it.

- Respond to these questions: Why is it so easy to pass up opportunities to serve others in small ways? Where have I not served Jesus by not serving others?

Option 5: Wrap It Up

Write out your answers to any questions that you didn't answer during your small group time.

LEARN A LITTLE MORE

Separate...sheep from the goats (Matthew 25:32)

In Jesus' time, sheep and goats normally grazed together during the day, but at night the herdsman separated them. In this passage, Jesus portrays himself as the shepherd of all people. At the end of this age, the Bible says Jesus will judge the world, separating nonbelievers from those who follow him.[1]

Righteous (25:37)

Since sin entered the world in the Garden of Eden, we have been separated from God. The resulting evil has led to pain, suffering, and injustice: People hunger, thirst, are treated as strangers, experience sickness, and so on. In this passage, those who receive eternal life are called "righteous." This means they have been made right with God, no longer live in slavery to sin, and therefore are united with God. The Bible is clear that we cannot achieve righteousness on our own—it is a gift from God: "In the LORD alone are righteousness and strength..." (Isaiah 45:24).

Eternal fire...eternal punishment (25:41,46)

Jesus did not leave a person's eternal destiny to question. If you truly believe in him, you naturally will seek ways to serve him. If you serve Jesus by serving others, your life will demonstrate a genuine faith in Jesus. If your motivation is only to care for yourself, it may mean you're not fully surrendered to

[1] D. A. Carson, "Matthew," The Expositor's Bible Commentary, New Testament, Frank E. Gaebelein, gen. ed., in Zondervan Reference Software, version 2.8 (Grand Rapids: Zondervan, 1998).

Jesus. Those who aren't fully surrendered to Jesus are subject to eternal separation from God—and God never wanted that in the first place. But because many people refuse to believe, follow, and love him, a place of eternal separation and misery does exist.

FOR DEEPER STUDY ON YOUR OWN

1. Check out James 2:15-26 to see the connection between faith and works.

2. Look up Revelation 20:11-15 and 21:1-5 for another picture of the future.

3. Ezekiel 34:17-24 describes another example of the separation of sheep and goats. What else do you learn from this passage?

4. In the Ezekiel passage, the inheritance of eternal life seems based on works—doing good things for others. Isn't this contrary to what the Bible teaches? (See Romans 3:22 and 1 John 5:13 for help.)

A WEEKLY REFLECTION

Take a minute to reflect on how well you've been doing in the following five areas of your spiritual life this week—a 10 means you did an amazing job. This reflection can serve as a spiritual gauge to help you consider some very important areas. This is for your personal evaluation and growth; it's NOT a test—no one else needs to see it.

FELLOWSHIP: CONNECTING YOUR HEART TO OTHERS

How well did I connect with other Christians?

1   2   3   4   5   6   7   8   9   10

DISCIPLESHIP: GROWING TO BE LIKE JESUS

How well did I take steps to grow spiritually and deepen my faith on my own?

1   2   3   4   5   6   7   8   9   10

MINISTRY: SERVING OTHERS IN LOVE

How well did I recognize opportunities to serve others and follow through?

1   2   3   4   5   6   7   8   9   10

EVANGELISM: SHARING YOUR STORY AND GOD'S STORY

How well did I engage in spiritual conversations with non-Christians?

1   2   3   4   5   6   7   8   9   10

WORSHIP: SURRENDERING YOUR LIFE TO HONOR GOD

How well did I focus on God's presence and honor him with my life? Was my relationship with God a primary focus?

1   2   3   4   5   6   7   8   9   10

When you finish, celebrate the areas where you feel good and consider how you can use those strengths to help others in their journey to be more like Jesus. You might also want to take time to identify some potential areas for growth.

SESSION 3
EXPRESSING COMPASSION

 LEADERS, READ PAGE 82.

It was the rainiest season Karen could remember. Her family lived at the top of a big hill, and for the most part their home was protected from flooding and water damage except for a few leaks. But at the bottom of the hill was a new family (the Millers) who had moved in a few months prior to the rain. By the time it ended, the Miller's house was completely flooded, all of their belongings were ruined, and everything inside was a huge mess. The house couldn't hold up under these flood conditions. Walls were literally falling down.

Karen felt bad for this family. She wanted to help in some way but knew most of their needs were financial—and as a teenager she just didn't have anything close to the funds the Millers needed. So instead she offered to baby-sit their young kids for free so they could work on the house without distractions. When Karen shared the prayer request in youth group, some other students also made themselves available to help—some brought meals, some brought tools, and some even got their parents involved! Before long, families began to contribute financially to the Millers. It was humbling for Karen to see others show compassion and take action beyond what she was able to do.

In this session, you'll see how compassion influences servanthood.

♥ FELLOWSHIP: CONNECTING YOUR HEART TO OTHERS

Goal: To share about your life and listen attentively to others, caring about what they share

1. If you were responsible for feeding 5,000 people, what would you serve? Make a menu.

2. Can you think of a crisis that makes you sad when you hear it on the news? (For example, car accidents, kidnappings, murders, natural disasters.)

🧠 DISCIPLESHIP: GROWING TO BE LIKE JESUS

Goal: To explore God's Word, gain biblical knowledge, and make personal applications

Compassion is the ability to see another's need and meet that need through action. Compassion isn't always a natural response. We might feel sorry for someone, but there's a big difference between pity and compassion!

Read Mark 6:30-44. (If you don't have a Bible, the passage is on page 89.)

1. This passage begins with the apostles reporting to Jesus all they had "done and taught." Mark 6:12-13 fills in

the picture: "They went out and preached that people should repent. They drove out many demons and anointed many sick people with oil and healed them." Why do you think Jesus wanted to leave the crowds behind and go to a solitary place with the disciples? Why didn't he send them back out to do more good acts of service?

2. What part does teaching play in this passage? (You may need to re-read the passage before you answer.)

3. In what way was the large crowd like "sheep without a shepherd"? What did the people need from Jesus?

4. What did it mean for Jesus to have compassion? How did Jesus show his compassion?

5. How does this passage show us that the disciples may have had less compassion than Jesus? Is there a connection between faith and compassion?

6. Is it possible to be too compassionate? Explain your answer.

7. Why did Jesus perform this miracle? What is its connection with compassion?

MINISTRY: SERVING OTHERS IN LOVE

Goal: To recognize and take advantage of opportunities to serve others

Compassion fatigue means you're tired of feeling and/or expressing compassion. Many people become numb to others' needs; it's easy to feel overwhelmed by all the hurt in the world. Television broadcasts endless images of suffering around the world: famine, war, injustice, killing, disease, poverty, AIDS. There is so much to be compassionate about.

1. Do you ever feel compassion fatigue? If so, how do you respond? If not, what do you think protects you from it?

2. Family and friends also have needs. Are the needs of those close to us ever as dramatic as those we see on TV?

EVANGELISM: SHARING YOUR STORY AND GOD'S STORY

Goal: To consider how the truths from this session might be applied to your relationships with unbelievers

1. When have you seen God meet a need in your life? Write down three examples of how God has met your needs in very real and practical ways.

2. Have you ever written down your faith story (or testimony)? If not, how might you use the answers to the above question in your testimony? How can a written testimony serve as an evangelistic tool?

🚶 WORSHIP: SURRENDERING YOUR LIFE TO HONOR GOD

Goal: To focus on God's presence

1. What does this passage mean? What does it look like?

   ## CARRY EACH OTHER'S BURDENS, AND IN THIS WAY YOU WILL FULFILL THE LAW OF CHRIST. (GALATIANS 6:2)

2. This session has focused on finding compassion for others. Is there anything happening in your life for which you'd like others to show compassion? Can you say something like this to your group? "I'm hurting because of _____. I really need others to support me."

3. How does supporting others' hurt and pain help you grow spiritually?

4. Close your time in prayer.

AT HOME THIS WEEK

Option 1: A Weekly Reflection

Take another self-evaluation that reflects five areas of your spiritual life (fellowship, discipleship, ministry, evangelism, and worship). See page 48.

Option 2: Daily Bible Readings

Check out the Bible reading plan on pages 109-110.

Option 3: Memory Verses

Memorize another verse from pages 114-115.

Option 4: Journaling

Choose one or more of the following options:

- Write down whatever is on your mind.
- Read your journal entry from last week and write a reflection about it.
- Finish these statements: I hurt for people who… I'm glad God feels compassion for me because…

Option 5: Wrap It Up

Write out your answers to any questions that you didn't answer during your small group time.

LEARN A LITTLE MORE

So they went away by themselves in a boat to a solitary place (Mark 6:32)

Jesus often retreated from the crowds for prayer and reflection. We see this several times in the Gospels. Since the disciples had just returned from their journeys, it was time for them all to get away for some rest and report to Jesus all that happened while they were doing ministry in other towns. Jesus knew their mission was important, but he also understood the power of solitude—and that if they were going to be effective ministers, they needed some alone time.

Compassion (6:34)

The Greek word *splagchnizomai* means "to be moved from the gut." Deep feelings of concern for others come from within. They move us to do something, not just feel something. Jesus both felt and acted on deep movements of compassion. Even more than multiplying the loaves and feeding the thousands, perhaps Jesus' greatest miracle in this passage was moving the disciples toward compassion for the multitudes.

Ate and were satisfied (6:42)

The feeding of the 5,000 recalls God's miraculous provision of food for the Israelites in the desert after they left Egypt.

God provided food called *manna* (bread from heaven) six days a week (Exodus 16), and when the people grumbled that they were sick of manna, God provided meat (Numbers 11). Moses complained to God, "Would they have enough if flocks and herds were slaughtered for them? Would they have enough if all the fish in the sea were caught for them?" (Numbers 11:22). Jesus provided more than enough at his miraculous meal.

The people's deepest need was for teaching; this is why Jesus had compassion on people who were lost. When the more immediate need of hunger arose, Jesus challenged his disciples to feed the crowd. Although they had just returned from a journey where they had performed miraculous signs, they didn't know how to care for the people. It's interesting that Jesus did the teaching and called the disciples to perform a miracle when many would say the spectacular multiplication of loaves and fish was more significant.

Men (6:44)

The word used for "men" in verse 44 is not in the generic sense (i.e., people in general), but specifically males. Matthew makes this clear by adding "besides women and children" (14:21) in his account. A crowd of 5,000 people was significant because the neighboring towns of Capernaum and Bethsaida numbered only about two or three thousand people total.

FOR DEEPER STUDY ON YOUR OWN

1. Read 2 Corinthians 1:3-7 to see God's compassion for us in action, and how we might use this to help others.

2. Read Mark 8:13-21. In this passage Jesus draws out another lesson from the feeding of the 5,000.

3. Compare John's account of feeding the crowd (John 6:1-13) to Mark's. What additional insights do you get about Jesus and his mission?

4. Read Exodus 16:1-26. How are Jesus' actions reflected in this story?

A WEEKLY REFLECTION

Take a minute to reflect on how well you've been doing in the following five areas of your spiritual life this week—a 10 means you did an amazing job. This reflection can serve as a spiritual gauge to help you consider some very important areas. This is for your personal evaluation and growth; it's NOT a test—no one else needs to see it.

FELLOWSHIP: CONNECTING YOUR HEART TO OTHERS'

How well did I connect with other Christians?

1 2 3 4 5 6 7 8 9 10

DISCIPLESHIP: GROWING TO BE LIKE JESUS

How well did I take steps to grow spiritually and deepen my faith on my own?

1 2 3 4 5 6 7 8 9 10

MINISTRY: SERVING OTHERS IN LOVE

How well did I recognize opportunities to serve others and follow through?

1 2 3 4 5 6 7 8 9 10

EVANGELISM: SHARING YOUR STORY AND GOD'S STORY

How well did I engage in spiritual conversations with non-Christians?

1 2 3 4 5 6 7 8 9 10

WORSHIP: SURRENDERING YOUR LIFE TO HONOR GOD

How well did I focus on God's presence and honor him with my life? Was my relationship with God a primary focus?

1   2   3   4   5   6   7   8   9   10

When you finish, celebrate the areas where you feel good and consider how you can use those strengths to help others in their journey to be more like Jesus. You might also want to take time to identify some potential areas for growth.

SESSION 4

THE HOLY SPIRIT

 LEADERS, READ PAGE 82.

Bethany teaches a children's Sunday school class at church each week. Even though she's been teaching for a few years, she still feels a little insecure. She's a lot younger than most of the other teachers, and because she's in high school, she doesn't feel as though she knows as much about the Bible as the adult teachers. She's not flashy or very creative with the weekly lessons, but the same children come back consistently because they know and love Bethany, and they know she loves them. She is always surprised at how the Holy Spirit can use her broken and messy words to accomplish something so much bigger than babysitting kids for an hour. The Holy Spirit continues to work through Bethany to help her teach—and reveal to her that her teaching is leading children to Jesus.

The Holy Spirit desires to work through us to serve others. Sometimes we feel him, and sometimes we don't, but he is always ready to come to our aid when service is needed.

♥ FELLOWSHIP: CONNECTING YOUR HEART TO OTHERS'

Goal: To share about your life and listen attentively to others, caring about what they share

1. When you hear the word *counselor*, do you have a positive or negative reaction? Explain your answer.

2. Who is someone you would go to for counsel? Why would you choose that person?

🧠 DISCIPLESHIP: GROWING TO BE LIKE JESUS

Goal: To explore God's Word, gain biblical knowledge, and make personal applications

The evening before Jesus was arrested and then crucified, he spent several hours preparing his disciples for life without him. He told them that he was going to his Father's house and leaving his followers on earth to continue his ministry. Of course, they would still need help beyond their human means. For this God would send them the Holy Spirit. Without the Holy Spirit none of us can serve as Jesus served. The Spirit is the power in a servant's heart.

Read John 14:15-27. (If you don't have a Bible, the passage is on page 90.)

1. In your opinion, what's the connection between loving someone and obeying someone? Is the connection the same in all relationships?

2. Why do you think the Holy Spirit is called the "counselor" and the "Spirit of truth"?

3. According to this passage, what's the connection between Jesus and God the Father? (You may need to re-

read the entire passage!)

4. Are there conditions in this passage for receiving the Spirit? If so, what are they?

5. In verse 17, Jesus says it's not possible for the world to accept the Spirit of truth. If this is true, how can someone begin to believe in Jesus?

6. In this passage, Jesus talks a lot about the relationship between his disciples and God the Father. Why do you think there's no specific mention of faith but a lot of talk about obedience?

7. What does it mean to be taught by the Holy Spirit? How do you know if the Holy Spirit is teaching you something? Can you give an example from your own life?

8. What is the overall tone of Jesus' message to his disciples? What was he trying to do?

9. Why do you think the disciples had "troubled hearts" and fear during this time? (Take a look at verse 27.)

MINISTRY: SERVING OTHERS IN LOVE

Goal: To recognize and take advantage of opportunities to serve others

The Holy Spirit desires to guide us in many areas—to know God more intimately, to love him more deeply, to serve him more faithfully. Often when we pursue wisdom from our Counselor, we want guidance toward personal fulfillment and happiness. But the Holy Spirit is much more interested in God's agenda than ours. Instead of selfish questions, the Holy Spirit wants us to ask questions like these:

- Where is God working around me?
- How can I contribute to what he's already doing?
- What might God want to accomplish through my life that won't bring any praise from people but only lead to God's glory?

1. Turn to page 92 where you'll see a page titled "God, How Can I Serve You?". Have someone pray briefly for the Holy Spirit to help, counsel, and teach you to become sensitive to his leading and to become more willing to serve.

   Then allow five minutes of silence for everyone to write. There are no rules about what you're to write—just write whatever is on your mind about serving. Try to be sensitive to what the Holy Spirit might be guiding you toward.

   Consider writing about one of the following:

   - Your questions about serving opportunities.
   - An opportunity to serve that's been on your mind or about obstacles you face in serving God.
   - What you think the Spirit might want you to know about service.
   - A prayer asking God to help you learn to follow the Spirit's lead.

2. Give group members an opportunity to share what they wrote.

EVANGELISM: SHARING YOUR STORY AND GOD'S STORY

Goal: To consider how the truths from this session might be applied to your relationships with unbelievers

1. How can we rely on the Holy Spirit during evangelism opportunities?

2. Read the passage below and then discuss how it might fit with evangelism.

"WHEN YOU ARE BROUGHT BEFORE SYNAGOGUES, RULERS, AND AUTHORITIES, DO NOT WORRY ABOUT HOW YOU WILL DEFEND YOURSELVES OR WHAT YOU WILL SAY, FOR THE HOLY SPIRIT WILL TEACH YOU AT THAT TIME WHAT YOU SHOULD SAY." (LUKE 12:11-12)

WORSHIP: SURRENDERING YOUR LIFE TO HONOR GOD

Goal: To focus on God's presence

1. What's one area of your life in which you need the Holy Spirit's counsel?

2. Share your answer with your group, and then pray for each other before you leave.

AT HOME THIS WEEK

Option 1: A Weekly Reflection

Take another self-evaluation that reflects five areas of your spiritual life (fellowship, discipleship, ministry, evangelism, and worship). See page 58.

Option 2: Daily Bible Readings

Check out the Bible reading plan on pages 109-110.

Option 3: Memory Verses

Memorize another verse from pages 114-115.

Option 4: Journaling

Choose one or more of the following options:

- Write down whatever is on your mind.
- Read your journal entry from last week and write a reflection about it.
- Respond to these questions: How can I explain the Holy Spirit to others? Based on what I learned in this session, how does the Holy Spirit work?

Option 5: Wrap It Up

Write out your answers to any questions that you didn't answer during your small group time.

LEARN A LITTLE MORE

If you love me, you will obey (John 14:15,23)

Love is more than good intentions surrounded by well-meaning words. Love is a choice, and it reflects our true values. Although this passage heavily emphasizes obedience, Jesus understood that actions are an expression of faith. To love Jesus is to love his teachings and live according to the path he reveals. Jesus came to bring full life (John 10:10), and we experience this when we obey him.

Counselor (14:16)

The Greek word for "counselor" is *paraclete*, which literally means "called to the side of." Some English translations use "comforter" instead. As believers, we are not alone in this world! In God's perfect plan, he has provided us with the Holy Spirit who acts as our aide, guiding us into a deeper relationship with God. The Holy Spirit teaches us new things and reminds us of the things we have already learned.

Spirit of truth (14:17)

The Holy Spirit also functions as a guide to what is true and right. The spirit sheds light on God's Word so we can understand and apply it.

The world will not see me any more (14:19)

The conversation in this passage took place the night before Jesus died. Although he defeated death and rose from the dead, Jesus only remained on earth for 40 days after his resurrection before ascending to heaven. So instead of seeing Jesus in the flesh for the rest of their lives, the disciples were given the Holy Spirit, sent from the Father to remind them (and us) of Jesus' teaching. The world saw God's love in his disciples—and eventually you and me—through the examples they lived.

Peace I leave with you (14:27)

The Holy Spirit is associated with peace. Our world brings fear and uncertainty. The Holy Spirit replaces these feelings with peace, a perfect confidence that God is in charge and knows what he's doing. In a Jewish context, *peace* means wholeness, completeness, God's best. The Holy Spirit is all of God's best for a Christian. It is out of this wholeness and completeness that we can serve others in healthy ways.

FOR DEEPER STUDY ON YOUR OWN

1. Read Acts 2:1-47 to see when the Holy Spirit came upon the disciples after Jesus ascended into heaven.

2. Read Galatians 5:25. What does it mean to keep in step with the Spirit?

3. In John 7:37-39, Jesus speaks of the Holy Spirit as "streams of living water" flowing within us. What does he mean? How does that help us serve him?

4. What connection between the Holy Spirit and service does Paul make in 1 Corinthians 12:1-11?

A WEEKLY REFLECTION

Take a minute to reflect on how well you've been doing in the following five areas of your spiritual life this week—a 10 means you did an amazing job. This reflection can serve as a spiritual gauge to help you consider some very important areas. This is for your personal evaluation and growth; it's NOT a test—no one else needs to see it.

FELLOWSHIP: CONNECTING YOUR HEART TO OTHERS'

How well did I connect with other Christians?

1   2   3   4   5   6   7   8   9   10

DISCIPLESHIP: GROWING TO BE LIKE JESUS

How well did I take steps to grow spiritually and deepen my faith on my own?

1   2   3   4   5   6   7   8   9   10

MINISTRY: SERVING OTHERS IN LOVE

How well did I recognize opportunities to serve others and follow through?

1   2   3   4   5   6   7   8   9   10

EVANGELISM: SHARING YOUR STORY AND GOD'S STORY

How well did I engage in spiritual conversations with non-Christians?

1   2   3   4   5   6   7   8   9   10

WORSHIP: SURRENDERING YOUR LIFE TO HONOR GOD

How well did I focus on God's presence and honor him with my life? Was my relationship with God a primary focus?

1   2   3   4   5   6   7   8   9   10

When you finish, celebrate the areas where you feel good and consider how you can use those strengths to help others in their journey to be more like Jesus. You might also want to take time to identify some potential areas for growth.

SESSION 5
SLAVES SET FREE...
TO SERVE AGAIN

 LEADERS, READ PAGE 82.

Easter was just a few weeks away. Amanda's friends were planning their yearly mission trip to Mexico. They were all excited to minister to adults and children in the villages south of the border. But Amanda wasn't excited. Everybody slept in tents, no one showered during the week, a lot of people came home sick, and it was a 10-hour bus ride back home. It wasn't anything she thought she would enjoy.

Amanda's friend Nicole was not a Christian but had heard about the trip. She wanted to go and asked Amanda if she would go with her to be a friendly face among so many people she didn't know. Amanda knew this was a great opportunity for Nicole to see the Holy Spirit at work. Amanda had seen people return from this trip every year committed to God and fired up to live for him. She knew it would be good for Nicole, but Amanda was torn because even though she was a Christian, she absolutely did *not* want to go on this mission trip! But she *did* want her friend to have an experience that might possibly change her life forever.

At first Amanda avoided praying about it because she knew what God was tugging at her to do. She also knew she sensed the Holy Spirit impress a message on her heart: "It's not about you, Amanda." God wanted Amanda to serve her friend and the Mexican community, and he wasn't going to let her selfishness or fear get in the way.

Amanda was reluctant, but she finally decided to go on the trip with Nicole. God used that trip in both of their lives. Amanda received so much satisfaction from loving the children in the villages that she began seriously considering children's ministry as a career.

Serving doesn't always feel natural or easy, but if we really want to serve our Master and Creator, we must be willing to serve when it's uncomfortable. In this session you'll be challenged by God's standards for servanthood.

♥ FELLOWSHIP: CONNECTING YOUR HEART TO OTHERS

Goal: To share about your life and listen attentively to others, caring about what they share

1. In your mind, what is the least appealing way to serve at church? (Think: babysitting children, cleaning toilets, scrubbing carpets, cleaning communion trays, and so on.)

2. What do you think is the most appealing way to serve at church—a way you've never served before?

DISCIPLESHIP: GROWING TO BE LIKE JESUS

Goal: To explore God's Word, gain biblical knowledge, and make personal applications

Jesus came to earth for a specific reason: "For even the Son of Man did not come to be served, but to serve, and to give his life as a ransom for many" (Mark 10:45). We are never more like Jesus than when we are serving others in his name. Many people believe it is going to church regularly or knowing a lot about the Bible that makes them true followers of Jesus. But the high standard Jesus set for his disciples (and for us today) was servanthood.

Read John 8:31-38. (If you don't have a Bible, the passage is on page 90.)

1. What does it mean to "hold" to the teaching of Jesus? Give a practical example from your own life.

2. What does it mean to be a disciple of Jesus?

3. Do you think it's possible to be a disciple without "holding" to the teachings of Jesus? Explain your answer.

4. Verse 32 speaks of freedom. What do you think that freedom is from? How could knowing the audience of John's Gospel affect the answer to this question?

5. How does knowing the truth lead to freedom? Give an example from your life when you learned the truth and were set free by it.

6. Verses 31-32 seem to set the following pattern: True discipleship leads to holding to Jesus' teaching, holding to his teaching leads to knowing the truth, and knowing the truth leads to being set free. What is the relationship between holding to Jesus' teaching and knowing the truth? Doesn't it make sense that you would know the truth first and then hold to the teaching?

7. According to this passage, what are the differences between a slave and a son?

8. Compare verses 31 and 37. Is there a contradiction here? If so, can it be resolved? How?

9. What does it mean to have "no room" for God's Word (verse 37)? What are some specific ways to make room?

10. Time to get personal: Do you feel like you have room for the truth of God's Word in your own life? How well are you "holding" (verse 31) to the teachings of Jesus?

MINISTRY: SERVING OTHERS IN LOVE

Goal: To recognize and take advantage of opportunities to serve others

The image of being set free from slavery is a powerful one. Try to imagine how terrible it must have been to be a slave at the mercy of your master's orders. History books tell us the details, but the humiliation and depth of pain that came with slavery can't be experienced through words on a page.

1. Can you think of any segment of society in which people are slaves to something? If so, can you name some examples?

2. You wouldn't have to look very hard to find someone in your community who's a slave to drugs or alcohol. These substances hold people captive; once addicted, it's difficult to get free. Is there a place in your community that helps those imprisoned by drugs and alcohol? Any rehabilitation centers that you know of? Is there anything your group can do to help these centers? List your ideas here.

3. Is there anyone in your church who feels called to help those held captive to the slavery of addiction? If so, who? What can your group do to encourage this person?

4. If you are planning a service project (from page 34), give an update. What's happened so far? What still needs to happen?

EVANGELISM: SHARING YOUR STORY AND GOD'S STORY

Goal: To consider how the truths from this session might be applied to your relationships with unbelievers

Prior to recognizing our need for God, we must be made aware of our sin. We all pretty much know we've sinned or done things that are wrong. But learning that the Bible calls it "sin" is the beginning of understanding that we're separated from a perfect and holy God. Once that picture becomes clear, we begin to desire freedom from sin and a deeper connection with God.

1. How would you explain sin to a non-Christian friend?

2. How would you respond if your friend said, "I'm not a slave to sin. I can stop sinning any time I want. I just don't want to."

3. Can you explain what the Bible teaches about sin? Look up these verses and discuss how you might graciously explain what the Bible teaches about sin.

   • Romans 6:17,22-23
   • Romans 8:3
   • 2 Corinthians 5:21

🚶 WORSHIP: SURRENDERING YOUR LIFE TO HONOR GOD

Goal: To focus on God's presence

If we are going to live as if we're free from sin and slaves to God's way, it requires daily surrender. This can only happen when we love and trust God as Master.

1. What's one area of your life that you find hardest to entrust to God? What's an area you find easy to entrust to God?

2. Pray for each other about what you've shared.

AT HOME THIS WEEK

Option 1: A Weekly Reflection

Take another self-evaluation that reflects five areas of your spiritual life (fellowship, discipleship, ministry, evangelism, and worship). See page 69.

Option 2: Daily Bible Readings

Check out the Bible reading plan on pages 109-110.

Option 3: Memory Verses

Memorize another verse from pages 114-115.

Option 4: Journaling

Choose one or more of the following options:

- Write down whatever is on your mind.
- Read your journal entry from last week and write a reflection about it.
- Respond to these questions: To what am I currently enslaved? How can I thank God for delivering me from slavery to my sin?

Option 5: Wrap It Up

Write out your answers to any questions that you didn't answer during your small group time.

LEARN A LITTLE MORE

To the Jews who believed...you are looking for a way to kill me (John 8:31-38)

It's not directly apparent from this passage that Jesus is speaking to a mixed crowd of Jews. The surrounding verses offer context (the clues) we need to arrive at this conclusion. In 8:12, Jesus is speaking "to the people," some of whom were Pharisees. He was teaching in the temple courts, which would have been filled with predominantly Jewish people. In 8:30, we see that "many put their faith" in Jesus, therefore his listeners were mixed—some believed in him, some didn't.

The truth will set you free (8:32)

The Jews lived according to the Law of Moses—which is essentially the first five books of the Old Testament. God revealed his holy law to Moses after he saved the Israelites from slavery in Egypt. The purpose of the law is to reveal our imperfections ("I would not have known what coveting really was if the law had not said, 'You shall not covet.'"—Romans 7:7). Although the law is perfect, it can only reveal our imperfections (sin); it does not lead to eternal life (Romans 7:10, 8:3). Knowledge of the law keeps us enslaved to sin, but the truth about Jesus—his sacrifice on the cross and victory in the resurrection—is controlled by the Spirit (Romans 8:9-13) and sets us free from sin if we believe (Romans 7:24-25, 8:1).

Abraham (8:33)

Abraham was called by God to leave his country and his family (see Genesis 12). God promised to make him and his descendants into a great nation—with so many people they would be like the stars in the sky and "impossible" to count. Abraham is famous for his faith in God, trusting God's commands through obedience (see Romans 4:1). The children of Abraham were first known as Israelites, later as Jews. But everyone who has faith in Jesus is a child of Abraham. God also promised "all the peoples on earth will be blessed through" Abraham (Genesis 12:3). This was a promise of the Messiah, Jesus, who would come to save the world and give life to all who believe (see Galatians 3:7-9).

FOR DEEPER STUDY ON YOUR OWN

1. To discover another teaching about discipleship, read Luke 14:25-35.

2. To learn more about the amazing life of Abraham, read Genesis 12-22.

3. What motivations does Paul offer for viewing yourself as God's slave in Romans 6:15-23? Is there anything in this passage that you don't understand?

4. How does Mary demonstrate the attitude of a slave or servant of God in Luke 1:26-38?

5. What do you think about the idea that you belong to God, that he bought you, and that you don't belong to yourself? Which parts of you agree with that? Which parts of you resist the idea? Explain.

A WEEKLY REFLECTION

Take a minute to reflect on how well you've been doing in the following five areas of your spiritual life this week—a 10 means you did an amazing job. This reflection can serve as a spiritual gauge to help you consider some very important areas. This is for your personal evaluation and growth; it's NOT a test—no one else needs to see it.

FELLOWSHIP: CONNECTING YOUR HEART TO OTHERS'
How well did I connect with other Christians?

1   2   3   4   5   6   7   8   9   10

DISCIPLESHIP: GROWING TO BE LIKE JESUS
How well did I take steps to grow spiritually and deepen my faith on my own?

1   2   3   4   5   6   7   8   9   10

MINISTRY: SERVING OTHERS IN LOVE

How well did I recognize opportunities to serve others and follow through?

1   2   3   4   5   6   7   8   9   10

EVANGELISM: SHARING YOUR STORY AND GOD'S STORY

How well did I engage in spiritual conversations with non-Christians?

1   2   3   4   5   6   7   8   9   10

WORSHIP: SURRENDERING YOUR LIFE TO HONOR GOD

How well did I focus on God's presence and honor him with my life? Was my relationship with God a primary focus?

1   2   3   4   5   6   7   8   9   10

When you finish, celebrate the areas where you feel good and consider how you can use those strengths to help others in their journey to be more like Jesus. You might also want to take time to identify some potential areas for growth.

SESSION 6

SERVING "THOSE KINDS" OF PEOPLE

 LEADERS, READ PAGE 82.

Jeff and Jason rode the bus to school their ninth grade year. The bus was loud and rowdy both to and from school every day. There was always a different girl to tease, a book to throw, or a guy to pick on. As far as guys to pick on, Peter was usually the unlucky one. Peter was different. He didn't look different, but he sure acted differently. He had a disease called Tourette's Syndrome. Peter sat alone right in the middle of the bus and rocked back and forth, sometimes shouting out strange, non-sensical words. The other students didn't know how to treat Peter and didn't understand him, so he was an easy target for jokes and rude comments behind his back—and to his face.

Jeff and Jason felt uneasy about teasing Peter. They knew he didn't understand all the jokes and the sarcasm that flew out around the bus. But they weren't sure what to do aside from not participating in the teasing.

After talking about the situation with their small group, they decided to have lunch with Peter one afternoon. It was

71

uncomfortable—they didn't know what to talk about, and it was hard to know how to act when Peter shouted uncontrollably. They listened to Peter stutter awkwardly through a story about what his family did for summer vacation—for the entire lunch period. Honestly, Jeff and Jason were a little relieved when lunch was over that day. But they decided to meet Peter for lunch once a week. They began to feel more at ease with him and even learned a few things about him. They also knew they were doing something that Jesus would do.

Sometimes it's easier to serve certain people than others, but God calls Christians to a higher standard—to serve everyone, *especially* those no one else likes or pays attention to. In this session you will be challenged to think about how to widen your circle of service.

♥ FELLOWSHIP: CONNECTING YOUR HEART TO OTHERS'

Goal: To share about your life and listen attentively to others, caring about what they share

Choose one of the following questions to answer.

1. Are there certain types of people you don't like? Don't name names, but if you feel safe enough to be honest, share the types of people who bug you (for example, cheerleaders, jocks, druggies, rich kids, and so on).

2. When you were in elementary school, did you have any enemies? Did you ever try to get back at them for things they did to you? If so, how?

🧠 DISCIPLESHIP: GROWING TO BE LIKE JESUS

Goal: To explore God's Word, gain biblical knowledge, and make personal applications

We live in a "me first" world where others come second. Often acts of service are really just acts—done in order to get something for ourselves in return, such as self-worth or popularity in the eyes of others. You might not think you are selfish, and if so, you may need to take another look at your motivation for serving. In these passages you may be challenged in new ways to serve others like Jesus did.

Before you start, write a one-sentence definition for serving. Share your definition with the group and discuss.

Read Luke 14:12-14. (If you don't have a Bible, the passage is on page 91.)

1. How would you change your definition of *serving* now that you've read this passage?

2. Respond to this statement: "True service is expressed to those who can neither help you nor hurt you."

3. Is there anything in this passage that motivates you to serve others? What is it, and why does it motivate you?

4. Is it possible to be too much of a servant? Explain why you think the way you do.

Read Luke 6:32-36. (If you don't have a Bible, the passage is on page 91.)

5. What is the most challenging aspect of this passage for you?

6. Why do you think God wants us to be servants?

7. Describe what your life would be like if you served in the way this passage describes. Get personal and be specific.

8. Reread verse 35. Does this mean we should give away everything we have no matter what? Explain your answer.

9. What does it mean that God is kind to the "ungrateful and the wicked" (verse 35)?

MINISTRY: SERVING OTHERS IN LOVE

Goal: To recognize and take advantage of opportunities to serve others

1. Who are the people in your world who come to mind when you think of "the poor, the crippled, the lame, the blind"?

2. Who are the people who come to mind when you think of those who don't love you, the ungrateful, and the wicked?

3. In what specific ways can you serve the people you identified in questions 1 and 2?

EVANGELISM: SHARING YOUR STORY AND GOD'S STORY

Goal: To consider how the truths from this session might be applied to your relationships with unbelievers

For five sessions you've been given the opportunity to think about non-Christian friends, discuss evangelism, consider your testimony, and pray for those who don't know Jesus.

Now, in your last session, try to bring some resolution to your heart for evangelism by completing the following sentences.

1. To care more about non-Christians, I must...

2. To take the time to write down my own faith story, I must...

3. Within the next month I'll be more evangelistic by...

🚶 WORSHIP: SURRENDERING YOUR LIFE TO HONOR GOD

Goal: To focus on God's presence

Will your group continue to meet after this session? If so, take a moment to write down the name of one friend you want to invite. Share that name with the group, and have everyone commit to pray that these people might come to be part of your group.

AT HOME THIS WEEK

Option 1: A Weekly Reflection
Take another self-evaluation that reflects five areas of your spiritual life (fellowship, discipleship, ministry, evangelism, and worship). See page 78.

Option 2: Daily Bible Readings
Check out the Bible reading plan on pages 109-110.

Option 3: Memory Verses
Memorize another verse from pages 114-115.

Option 4: Journaling
Choose one or more of the following options:

Since this is the last time your group will be together with this particular book as your guide, make sure you take some time to discuss what will happen to your group next. If you want to continue to study the incredible life and teachings of Jesus, there are a total of six books in this series.

- Write down whatever is on your mind.
- Read your journal entry from last week and write a reflection about it.
- Complete these questions: What kind of person do I find it difficult to serve? Sometimes I feel guilty because I make fun of this type of person...

Option 5: Wrap It Up

Write out your answers to any questions that you didn't answer during your small group time.

LEARN A LITTLE MORE

The poor, the crippled, the lame, the blind (Luke 14:13)

In Jesus' day, "respectable people" often avoided the disabled because they viewed them as inferior—even impure. The law for priests in Leviticus 21:16-21, which says that priests had to be physically perfect as a symbol of God's perfection, was misinterpreted to include ordinary men and women. People thought disabilities indicated spiritual flaws and believed that they were evidence of God's judgment. In John 9:2, when encountering a blind man, the disciples asked Jesus, "Rabbi, who sinned, this man or his parents, that he was born blind?" Jesus' response was, "Neither" (John 9:3). Jesus urged his followers to extend hospitality to the needy, the disabled, and to those whose lives seemed a mess.

Resurrection of the righteous (14:14)

At the end of time, the righteous (those who are right with God through faith in Jesus) will be raised from the dead to live eternally with God in heaven. Keeping an eternal perspective is important for living a holy life today (Matthew 25:46). One day, God will judge the world. Those who have faith in Jesus will face a second judgment where we will be rewarded according to our actions (1 Corinthians 3:12-15). Salvation is by faith, but God does provide rewards in heaven for faithfulness we show today.

Repaid at the resurrection (14:14)

Jesus promises rewards to those who serve on his behalf, but he doesn't spell out the details of those rewards. In 1 Corinthians 3:10-15, Paul suggests that anything we've done that is good and rooted in Jesus will last into eternity and bring us a reward. If we long to make our lives count, service is the way to go.

FOR DEEPER STUDY ON YOUR OWN

1. Read Philippians 2:1-11 for a challenge to be humble like Jesus and to serve like he did.

2. Check out Galatians 5:13-18 to see what it means to serve in the power of the Holy Spirit.

3. Read Colossians 3:12-14 for some practical ideas on how we can serve others.

4. Read 1 Corinthians 3:10-15. What kinds of work or service do you think qualify as gold, silver, or costly stones? What do you think it will be like for those who are saved but whose entire work on earth is consumed by flames because it has no lasting worth?

5. What else can you learn about our eternal destiny from 1 Corinthians 15:42-44,51-54; 2 Corinthians 5:1-10; and 1 Thessalonians 4:16-17? How motivating is it for you here and now to think about your eternal destiny?

A WEEKLY REFLECTION

Take a minute to reflect on how well you've been doing in the following five areas of your spiritual life this week—a 10 means you did an amazing job. This reflection can serve as a spiritual gauge to help you consider some very important areas. This is for your personal evaluation and growth; it's NOT a test—no one else needs to see it.

FELLOWSHIP: CONNECTING YOUR HEART TO OTHERS'

How well did I connect with other Christians?

1   2   3   4   5   6   7   8   9   10

DISCIPLESHIP: GROWING TO BE LIKE JESUS

How well did I take steps to grow spiritually and deepen my faith on my own?

1   2   3   4   5   6   7   8   9   10

MINISTRY: SERVING OTHERS IN LOVE

How well did I recognize opportunities to serve others and follow through?

1   2   3   4   5   6   7   8   9   10

EVANGELISM: SHARING YOUR STORY AND GOD'S STORY

How well did I engage in spiritual conversations with non-Christians?

1   2   3   4   5   6   7   8   9   10

APPENDICES

SMALL GROUP LEADER CHECKLIST

- **Read through "For Small Group Leaders: How to Best Use this Material"** (see pages 83-86). This is very important—familiarizing yourself with it will help you understand content and how to best manage your time.

- **Read through all the questions in the session that you'll be leading.** The questions are a guide for you to help students grow spiritually. Think through which questions are best for your group. Remember, no curriculum author knows your students better than you do! Just a small amount of preparation on your part will help you manage the time you'll have with your group. Based on the amount of time you'll have in your small group, circle the questions you will discuss as a group. Decide what (if anything) you will assign at the end of the session (things like homework, snacks, group project, and so on).

- **Remember that the questions in this book don't always have obvious, neat, tidy answers.** Some are purposely written to cause good discussion without a specific "right" answer. Often questions (and answers) will lead to more questions.

- **Make sure you have enough books for your students and a few extra in case your students invite friends.** (Note: It's vital for your group to decide during the first session whether you can invite friends to join your group. If not, encourage your group to think of friends they can invite if you go through the next EXPERIENCING CHRIST TOGETHER book in this series.)

- **Read the material included in this appendix.** It's filled with information that will benefit your group and your student ministry. This appendix alone is a great reference for students—familiarize yourself with the tools here so you can offer them to students.

- **Submit your leadership and your group to God.** Ask God to provide you with insight into how to lead your group, patience to do so, and courage to speak truth in love when needed.

FOR SMALL GROUP LEADERS: HOW TO BEST USE THIS MATERIAL

This book was written more as a guidebook than a workbook. In most workbooks, you're supposed to answer every question and fill in all the blanks. In this book, there are lots of questions and plenty of blank space. Explain to your students that this isn't a school workbook—they're not graded on how much they've written.

The number-one rule for this curriculum is that there are no rules apart from the ones you decide to use. Every small group is unique and will figure out its own style and system. (The exception is when the lead youth worker establishes a guideline for all the groups to follow. In that case, respect your leader's guidelines.)

If you need a guide to get you started until you navigate your own way, here's a way to adapt the material for a 60-minute session.

Introduction (4 minutes)

Begin each session with one student reading the Small Group Covenant (see page 18). This becomes a constant reminder of why you'll be doing what you're doing. Then have another student read the opening paragraphs of the session you'll be discussing. Allow different students to take turns reading these two opening pieces.

Connecting (10 minutes)

This section can take 45 minutes if you're not careful! You'll need to stay on task to keep this segment short—consider giving students a specific amount of time and holding them to it. It's always better to leave students wanting more time for discussion than to leave them bored.

Growing (25 minutes)

Read God's Word and work through the questions you think will be best for your group. This section definitely has more questions than you're able to discuss in the allotted time. Before the small group begins, take some time to read through the questions and choose the best ones for your group. You may also want to add questions of your own. If someone forgets a Bible, we've provided the Scripture passages for each session in the appendix.

The questions in this book don't always have obvious, neat, tidy answers. Some are purposely written to cause good discussion without a specific "right" answer. Often questions (and answers) will lead to more questions.

If your small group is biblically mature, this section won't be too difficult. However, if your group struggles with these questions, make sure you sift through them and focus on the few questions that will help drive the message home. Also, you might want to encourage your group to answer the remaining questions on their own.

Serving and Sharing (10 minutes)

If you're pressed for time, you may choose to skip one of these two sections. If you do need to skip one due to time constraints, group members can finish the section on their own during the week. Don't feel guilty about passing over a section. **One of the strengths of this material is the built-in, intentional repetition in every session. You will have other opportunities to discuss that biblical purpose.** (Again, that's the main reason for spending a few minutes before your group meets to read through all the questions and pick the best ones for your group.)

Surrendering (10 minutes)

We always want to end the lesson with a focus on God and a specific time of prayer. You'll have several options but feel free to default to your group's comfort level.

Closing Challenge (1 minute)

Encourage students to pick one option each from the "At Home This Week" section to complete on their own. The more students initiate and develop the habit of spending time with God, the healthier their spiritual journeys will be. We've found that students have plenty of unanswered questions that they will consider on their own time. **Keep in mind that the main goal of this book is building spiritual growth in community—not to get your students to answer every question correctly.** Remember that this is your small group, your time, and the questions will always be there. Use them, ignore them, or assign them for personal study during the week—but don't feel pressure to follow this curriculum exactly or "grade" your group's biblical knowledge.

Finally, remember that questions are a great way to get students connected to one another and God's Word. You don't have to have all the answers.

Suggestions for Existing Small Groups

If your small group has been meeting for a while, and you've already established comfortable relationships, you can jump right into the material. But make sure you take the following actions, even if you're a well-established group:

- Read through the "Small Group Covenant" on page 18 and make additions or adjustments as necessary.

- Read the "Prayer Request Guidelines" together (page 127). You can maximize the group's time by following them.

- Before each meeting, consider whether you'll assign material to be completed (or at least thought through) before your next meeting.

- Familiarize yourself with all the "At Home This Week" options at the end of each session. They are explained in detail near the end of Session 1 (page 24), and then briefly summarized at the end of the other five sessions.

Although handling business like this can seem cumbersome or unnecessary to an existing group, these foundational steps can save you from headaches later on because you took the time to create an environment conducive to establishing deep relationships.

Suggestions for New Small Groups

If your group is meeting together for the first time, jumping right into the first session may not be your best option. You may want to meet as a group before you begin going through the book so you can get to know each other better. To prepare for the first gathering, read and follow the "Suggestions for Existing Groups" mentioned previously.

Spend some time getting to know each other with icebreaker questions. Several are listed here. Pick one or two that will work best for your group or use your own. The goal is to break ground so you can plant the seeds of healthy relationships.

1. What's your name, school, grade, and favorite class in school? (Picking your least favorite class is too easy.)

2. Tell the group a brief (basic) history of your family. What's your family life like? How many brothers and sisters do you have? Which family members are you closest to?

3. What's one thing about yourself that you really like?

4. Everyone has little personality quirks—traits that make each one of us unique. What are yours?

5. Why did you choose to be a part of this small group?

6. What do you hope to get out of this small group? How do you expect it to help you?

7. What do you think it will take to make our small group work well?

Need some teaching help?

Companion DVDs are available for each EXPERIENCING CHRIST TOGETHER book. These DVDs contain teaching segments you can use to supplement each session. Play them before your discussion begins or just prior to the "Discipleship" section in each session. The DVDs aren't required, but they are a great complement and supplement to the small group material. These are available from www.youthspecialties.com.

SCRIPTURE PASSAGES

Session 1

Mark 10:36-45

[36] "What do you want me to do for you?" he asked.

[37] They replied, "Let one of us sit at your right and the other at your left in your glory."

[38] "You don't know what you are asking," Jesus said. "Can you drink the cup I drink or be baptized with the baptism I am baptized with?"

[39] "We can," they answered.

Jesus said to them, "You will drink the cup I drink and be baptized with the baptism I am baptized with, [40]but to sit at my right or left is not for me to grant. These places belong to those for whom they have been prepared."

[41] When the ten heard about this, they became indignant with James and John. [42]Jesus called them together and said, "You know that those who are regarded as rulers of the Gentiles lord it over them, and their high officials exercise authority over them. [43]Not so with you. Instead, whoever wants to become great among you must be your servant, [44]and whomever wants to be first must be slave of all. [45]For even the Son of Man did not come to be served, but to serve, and to give his life as a ransom for many."

Philippians 2:6-11

[6] Who, being in very nature God,

did not consider equality with God something to be grasped,

[7] but made himself nothing,

taking the very nature of a servant,

being made in human likeness.

[8] And being found in appearance as a man,

he humbled himself

and became obedient to death—

even death on a cross!

⁹Therefore God exalted him to the highest place

and gave him the name that is above every name,

¹⁰that at the name of Jesus every knee should bow,

in heaven and on earth and under the earth,

¹¹and every tongue confess that Jesus Christ is Lord,

to the glory of God the Father.

Session 2

Matthew 25:31-46

³¹When the Son of Man comes in his glory, and all the angels with him, he will sit on his throne in heavenly glory. ³²All the nations will be gathered before him, and he will separate the people one from another as a shepherd separates the sheep from the goats. ³³He will put the sheep on his right and the goats on his left.

³⁴ "Then the King will say to those on his right, 'Come, you who are blessed by my Father; take your inheritance, the kingdom prepared for you since the creation of the world. ³⁵For I was hungry and you gave me something to eat, I was thirsty and you gave me something to drink, I was a stranger and you invited me in, ³⁶I needed clothes and you clothed me, I was sick and you looked after me, I was in prison and you came to visit me.'

³⁷ "Then the righteous will answer him, 'Lord, when did we see you hungry and feed you, or thirsty and give you something to drink? ³⁸When did we see you a stranger and invite you in, or needing clothes and clothe you? ³⁹When did we see you sick or in prison and go to visit you?'

⁴⁰ "The King will reply, 'I tell you the truth, whatever you did for one of the least of these brothers of mine, you did for me.'

⁴¹ "Then he will say to those on his left, 'Depart from me, you who are cursed, into the eternal fire prepared for the devil and his angels. ⁴²For I was hungry and you gave me nothing to eat, I was thirsty and you gave me nothing to drink, ⁴³I was a stranger and you did not invite me in, I needed clothes and you did not clothe me, I was sick and in prison and you did not look after me.'

⁴⁴ "They also will answer, 'Lord, when did we see you hungry or thirsty or

a stranger or needing clothes or sick or in prison, and did not help you?'

⁴⁵ "He will reply, 'I tell you the truth, whatever you did not do for one of the least of these, you did not do for me.'

⁴⁶ "Then they will go away to eternal punishment, but the righteous to eternal life."

Session 3

Mark 6:30-44

³⁰The apostles gathered around Jesus and reported to him all they had done and taught. ³¹Then, because so many people were coming and going that they did not even have a chance to eat, he said to them, "Come with me by yourselves to a quiet place and get some rest."

³²So they went away by themselves in a boat to a solitary place. ³³But many who saw them leaving recognized them and ran on foot from all the towns and got there ahead of them. ³⁴When Jesus landed and saw a large crowd, he had compassion on them, because they were like sheep without a shepherd. So he began teaching them many things.

³⁵By this time it was late in the day, so his disciples came to him. "This is a remote place," they said, "and it's already very late. ³⁶Send the people away so they can go to the surrounding countryside and villages and buy themselves something to eat."

³⁷But he answered, "You give them something to eat."

They said to him, "That would take eight months of a man's wages! Are we to go and spend that much on bread and give it to them to eat?"

³⁸ "How many loaves do you have?" he asked. "Go and see."

When they found out, they said, "Five—and two fish."

³⁹Then Jesus directed them to have all the people sit down in groups on the green grass. ⁴⁰So they sat down in groups of hundreds and fifties. ⁴¹Taking the five loaves and the two fish and looking up to heaven, he gave thanks and broke the loaves. Then he gave them to his disciples to set before the people. He also divided the two fish among them all. ⁴²They all ate and were satisfied, ⁴³and the disciples picked up twelve basketfuls of broken pieces of bread and fish. ⁴⁴The number of the men who had eaten was five thousand.

Session 4

John 14:15-27

[15] "If you love me, you will obey what I command. [16]And I will ask the Father, and he will give you another Counselor to be with you forever—[17]the Spirit of truth. The world cannot accept him, because it neither sees him nor knows him. But you know him, for he lives with you and will be in you. [18]I will not leave you as orphans; I will come to you. [19]Before long, the world will not see me anymore, but you will see me. Because I live, you also will live. [20]On that day you will realize that I am in my Father, and you are in me, and I am in you. [21]Whoever has my commands and obeys them, he is the one who loves me. He who loves me will be loved by my Father, and I too will love him and show myself to him."

[22]Then Judas (not Judas Iscariot) said, "But, Lord, why do you intend to show yourself to us and not to the world?"

[23]Jesus replied, "If anyone loves me, he will obey my teaching. My Father will love him, and we will come to him and make our home with him. [24]He who does not love me will not obey my teaching. These words you hear are not my own; they belong to the Father who sent me.

[25] "All this I have spoken while still with you. [26]But the Counselor, the Holy Spirit, whom the Father will send in my name, will teach you all things and will remind you of everything I have said to you. [27]Peace I leave with you; my peace I give you. I do not give to you as the world gives. Do not let your hearts be troubled and do not be afraid."

Session 5

John 8:31-38

[31]To the Jews who had believed him, Jesus said, "If you hold to my teaching, you are really my disciples. [32]Then you will know the truth, and the truth will set you free."

[33]They answered him, "We are Abraham's descendants and have never been slaves of anyone. How can you say that we shall be set free?"

[34]Jesus replied, "I tell you the truth, everyone who sins is a slave to sin. [35]Now a slave has no permanent place in the family, but a son belongs to it forever. [36]So if the Son sets you free, you will be free indeed. [37]I know you are Abraham's descendants. Yet you are ready to kill me, because you have no room for my word. [38]I am telling you what I have seen in the Father's presence, and you do what you have heard from your father."

Session 6

Luke 14:12-14

[12]Then Jesus said to his host, "When you give a luncheon or dinner, do not invite your friends, your brothers or relatives, or your rich neighbors; if you do, they may invite you back and so you will be repaid. [13]But when you give a banquet, invite the poor, the crippled, the lame, the blind, [14]and you will be blessed. Although they cannot repay you, you will be repaid at the resurrection of the righteous."

Luke 6:32-36

[32]"If you love those who love you, what credit is that to you? Even 'sinners' love those who love them. [33]And if you do good to those who are good to you, what credit is that to you? Even 'sinners' do that. [34]And if you lend to those from whom you expect repayment, what credit is that to you? Even 'sinners' lend to 'sinners,' expecting to be repaid in full. [35]But love your enemies, do good to them, and lend to them without expecting to get anything back. Then your reward will be great, and you will be sons of the Most High, because he is kind to the ungrateful and wicked. [36]Be merciful, just as your Father is merciful."

MINISTRY ACTIVITY FOR SESSION 4
"GOD, HOW CAN I SERVE YOU?"

Consider writing about one of the following:

- Your questions about serving opportunities.
- An opportunity to serve that's on your mind or about obstacles you face in serving God.
- What you think the Spirit might want you to know about service.
- A prayer asking God to help you learn to follow the Spirit's lead.

WHO IS JESUS?

Jesus is God

The high priest said to him, "I charge you under oath by the living God: Tell us if you are the Christ, the Son of God." "Yes, it is as you say," Jesus replied. (Matthew 26:63-64)

Jesus became a person

The Word [Jesus] became flesh and made his dwelling among us. (John 1:14)

Jesus taught with authority

They were amazed at his teaching, for he taught as one who had real authority—quite unlike the teachers of religious law. (Mark 1:22)

Jesus healed the sick

Jesus went throughout Galilee, teaching in their synagogues, preaching the good news of the kingdom, and healing every disease and sickness among the people. (Matthew 4:23)

Jesus befriended outcasts

That night Matthew invited Jesus and his disciples to be his dinner guests, along with his fellow tax collectors and many other notorious sinners. The Pharisees were indignant. "Why does your teacher eat with such scum?" they asked his disciples. (Matthew 9:10-11)

Jesus got angry with religious oppressors

How terrible it will be for you teachers of religious law and you Pharisees. Hypocrites! You are like whitewashed tombs—beautiful on the outside but filled on the inside with dead people's bones and all sorts of impurity. (Matthew 23:27)

Jesus was persecuted

The chief priests and the whole Sanhedrin were looking for false evidence against Jesus so that they could put him to death. But they did not find any, though many false witnesses came forward. Finally two came forward. (Matthew 26:59-60)

Jesus was tempted in every way

… for he [Jesus] faced all of the same temptations we do… (Hebrews 4:15)

Jesus never sinned

… he [Jesus] did not sin. (Hebrews 4:15)

But you know that he [Jesus] appeared so that he might take away our sins. And in him is no sin. (1 John 3:5)

Jesus died, rose from the dead, and continues to live to this day

But Christ has indeed been raised from the dead… (1 Corinthians 15:20)

Jesus made it possible to have a relationship with God

For God so loved the world that he gave his one and only Son, that whoever believes in him shall not perish but have eternal life. For God did not send his Son into the world to condemn the world, but to save the world through him. (John 3:16-17)

Jesus can sympathize with our struggles

This High Priest of ours understands our weaknesses… (Hebrews 4:15)

Jesus loves us

May you experience the love of Christ, though it is so great you will never fully understand it. (Ephesians 3:19)

Sound good? Looking for more?

Getting to know Jesus is the best thing you can do with your life. He WON'T let you down. He knows everything about you and LOVES you more than you can imagine!

A SUMMARY OF THE LIFE OF JESUS

The Incarnation

Fully divine and fully human, God sent his son, Jesus, to the earth to bring salvation into the world for everyone who believes. *Read John 1:4.*

John the Baptist

A relative to Jesus, John was sent "to make ready a people prepared for the Lord." He called Israel to repentance and baptized people in the Jordan River. *Read Luke 3:3.*

The baptism and temptation of Jesus

After John baptized him, Jesus went into the desert for 40 days in preparation for his ministry. He faced Satan and resisted the temptation he offered by quoting Scripture. *Read Matthew 4:4.*

Jesus begins his ministry

The world's most influential person taught with authority, healed with compassion, and inspired with miracles. *Read Luke 4:15.*

Jesus' model of discipleship

Jesus called everyone to follow him—without reservation—and to love God and others. *Read Luke 9:23, 57-62.*

The opposition

The religious "upper class" opposed Jesus, seeking to discredit him in the eyes of the people. Jesus criticized their hypocrisy and love of recognition. *Read Matthew 23:25.*

The great "I Am"

Jesus claimed to be the bread of life; the light of the world; the good shepherd; and the way, the truth, and the life. Each of these titles reveals essential truth about who he is. *Read John 14:6.*

The great physician

His words brought conviction and comfort; his actions shouted to the world his true nature. Healing the sick, Jesus demonstrated his power and authority by helping people where they needed it most so they might accept the truth. *Read Matthew 14:14.*

The great forgiver

Humanity's deepest need is forgiveness and freedom from the guilt of the past—which separates us from God. Only God has the power to forgive, and Jesus further demonstrated his divinity by forgiving the guilty. *Read Matthew 9:6.*

The disciples

Jesus chose 12 ordinary men to change the world. They weren't rich, powerful, or influential. They had shady pasts, often made huge mistakes, and were filled with doubts. In spite of these things, Jesus used them to build his church. *Read Mark 3:14.*

The final night

On the night before his death, Jesus spent the time preparing his disciples, and he spent time alone. Obedient to the Father, Jesus was committed to go to the cross to pay the penalty for our sins. *Read Mark 14:32 ff.*

The Crucifixion

Jesus died a real death on the cross for the sins of the world. His ultimate sacrifice is something all believers should remember often. *Read John 19:30.*

The Resurrection

After dying on the cross, Jesus was raised from the dead by God's power. This miracle has never been disproved and validates everything Jesus taught. *Read 1 Corinthians 15:55.*

Want a more detailed chronology of Jesus' life and ministry on earth? Check out these two Web sites:

http://www.bookofjesus.com/bojchron.htm

http://mb-soft.com/believe/txh/gospgosp.htm

SMALL GROUP ROSTER

NAME	E-MAIL	PHONE	ADDRESS / CITY / ZIP CODE	SCHOOL/GRADE

HOW TO KEEP YOUR GROUP FROM BECOMING A CLIQUE

We all want to belong—God created us to be connected in community with one another. But the same drive that creates healthy community can also create negative community, often called a clique. A clique isn't just a group of friends—it's a group of friends uninterested in anyone outside their group. Cliques result in pain for those who are excluded.

If you read the second paragraph of the introduction (page 7), you see the words *spiritual community* used to describe your small group. If your small group becomes a clique, it's an unspiritual community. You have a clique when the biblical purpose of fellowship turns inward. That's ugly. It's the opposite of what God intended the body of Christ to be. Here's why:

- Cliques make your youth ministry look bad.
- Cliques make your small group appear immature.
- Cliques hurt the feelings of excluded people.
- Cliques contradict the value God places on each person.
- Few things are as unappealing as a youth ministry filled with cliques.

Many leaders avoid using small groups as a way toward spiritual growth because they fear their groups will become cliques. But when they're healthy, small groups can improve your youth ministry's well-being, friendliness, and depth. The apostle Paul reminds us, "Be wise in the way you act toward outsiders; make the most of every opportunity" (Colossians 4:5).

Here are some ideas for being wise and preventing your small group from turning into a clique:

Be Aware

Learn to recognize when outsiders are uncomfortable with your group. It's easy to forget when you're an insider how bad it feels to be an outsider.

Reach Out

Once you're aware of someone feeling left out, make efforts to be friendly. Smile, shake hands, say hello, ask him or her to sit with you or your group, and ask simple yet personal questions. An outsider may come across as defensive, so be as accepting as possible.

Launch New Small Groups

Any small group with the attitude of "us four and no more" has become a clique. A time will come when your small group should launch into multiple small groups if it gets too big—because the bigger a small group gets, the less healthy it becomes. If your small group understands this, you can foster a culture of growth and fellowship.

For Students Only

Small group members expect adult leaders to confront them for acting like a clique. But instead of waiting for an adult to make the move, shock everyone by stepping up and challenging what you know is destructive. Take a risk. Be a spokesperson for your youth ministry and your student peers by leading the way. Be part of a small group that isn't cliquey and don't be afraid to challenge those who are.

SPIRITUAL HEALTH ASSESSMENT

Evaluating your spiritual journey is important—that's why we've encouraged you to take a brief survey at the end of each session. The following few pages are simply longer versions of that short evaluation tool.

Your spiritual journey will take you to low spots as well as high places. Spiritual growth is not a smooth incline—a loopy roller coaster is more like it. When you regularly consider your life, you'll develop an awareness of God's Spirit working in you. Evaluate. Think. Learn. Grow.

The assessment in this section is a tool, not a test. The purpose of this tool is to help you evaluate where you are in your faith journey. No one is perfect, so don't worry about your score. It won't be published in your church bulletin. Be honest so you have an accurate idea of how you're doing.

When you finish, celebrate the areas where you're relatively healthy and think about how you can use your strengths to help others on their spiritual journeys. Then think of ways your group members can help one another improve weak areas through support and example.

FELLOWSHIP: CONNECTING YOUR HEART TO OTHERS'

1. I meet consistently with a small group of Christians.

1	2	3	4	5
POOR				OUTSTANDING

2. I'm connected to other Christians who hold me accountable.

1	2	3	4	5
POOR				OUTSTANDING

3. I can talk with my small group leader when I need help, advice, or support.

1	2	3	4	5
POOR				OUTSTANDING

4. My Christian friends are a significant source of strength and stability in my life.

1	2	3	4	5
POOR				OUTSTANDING

5. I regularly pray for others in my small group outside of our meetings.

1	2	3	4	5
POOR				OUTSTANDING

6. I have resolved all conflicts with other people—both Christians and non-Christians.

1	2	3	4	5
POOR				OUTSTANDING

7. I've done all I possibly can to be a good son or daughter and brother or sister.

1	2	3	4	5
POOR				OUTSTANDING

TOTAL:_____

Take time to answer the following questions to further evaluate your spiritual health. You can do this after your small group meets if you don't have time during the meeting. If you need help with this, schedule a time with your small group leader to talk about your spiritual health.

8. List the three most significant relationships you have right now. Why are these people important to you?

9. How would you describe the benefit from being in fellowship with other Christians?

10. Do you have an accountability partner? If so, what have you been doing to hold each other accountable? If not, how can you get one?

DISCIPLESHIP: GROWING TO BE LIKE JESUS

11. I have regular times of conversation with God.

1	2	3	4	5
POOR				OUTSTANDING

12. I'm closer to God this month than I was last month.

1	2	3	4	5
POOR				OUTSTANDING

13. I'm making better decisions this month compared to last month.

1	2	3	4	5
POOR				OUTSTANDING

14. I regularly attend church services and grow spiritually as a result.

1	2	3	4	5
POOR				OUTSTANDING

15. I consistently honor God with my finances through giving.

1	2	3	4	5
POOR				OUTSTANDING

16. I regularly study the Bible on my own.

1	2	3	4	5
POOR				OUTSTANDING

17. I regularly memorize Bible verses or passages.

1	2	3	4	5
POOR				OUTSTANDING

TOTAL:_____

Take time to answer the following questions to further evaluate your spiritual health. You can do this after your small group meets if you don't have time during the meeting. If you need help with this, schedule a time with your small group leader to talk about your spiritual health.

18. What books or chapters from the Bible have you read during the last month?

19. What has God been teaching you lately from Scripture?

20. What was the last verse you memorized? When did you memorize it? Describe the last time a memorized Bible verse helped you.

MINISTRY: SERVING OTHERS IN LOVE

21. I am currently serving in some ministry capacity.

1	2	3	4	5
POOR				OUTSTANDING

22. I'm effectively ministering where I'm serving.

1	2	3	4	5
POOR				OUTSTANDING

23. Generally I have a humble attitude when I serve others.

1	2	3	4	5
POOR				OUTSTANDING

24. I understand God has created me as a unique individual, and he has a special plan for my life.

1	2	3	4	5
POOR				OUTSTANDING

25. When I help others, I typically don't look for anything in return.

1	2	3	4	5
POOR				OUTSTANDING

26. My family and friends consider me generally unselfish.

1	2	3	4	5
POOR				OUTSTANDING

27. I'm usually sensitive to others' hurts and respond in a caring way.

1	2	3	4	5
POOR				OUTSTANDING

TOTAL:_____

Take time to answer the following questions to further evaluate your spiritual health. You can do this after your small group meets if you don't have time during the meeting. If you need help with this, schedule a time with your small group leader to talk about your spiritual health.

28. If you're currently serving in a ministry, why are you serving? If not, what's kept you from getting involved?

29. What spiritual lessons have you learned while serving?

30. What frustrations have you experienced as a result of serving?

EVANGELISM: SHARING YOUR STORY AND GOD'S STORY

31. I regularly pray for my non-Christian friends.

1	2	3	4	5
POOR				OUTSTANDING

32. I invite my non-Christian friends to church.

1	2	3	4	5
POOR				OUTSTANDING

33. I talk about my faith with others.

1	2	3	4	5
POOR				OUTSTANDING

34. I pray for opportunities to share what Jesus has done in my life.

1	2	3	4	5
POOR				OUTSTANDING

35. People know I'm a Christian because of what I do, not just because of what I say.

1	2	3	4	5
POOR				OUTSTANDING

36. I feel strong compassion for non-Christians.

1	2	3	4	5
POOR				OUTSTANDING

37. I have written my testimony and am ready to share it.

1	2	3	4	5
POOR				OUTSTANDING

TOTAL:_____

Take time to answer the following questions to further evaluate your spiritual health. You can do this after your small group meets if you don't have time during the meeting. If you need help with this, schedule a time with your small group leader to talk about your spiritual health.

38. Describe any significant spiritual conversations you've had with non-Christians during the last month.

39. Have non-Christians ever challenged your faith? If yes, describe how.

40. Describe some difficulties you've faced when sharing your faith.

41. What successes have you experienced recently in personal evangelism? (Success isn't limited to bringing people to salvation directly. Helping someone take a step closer at any point on his or her spiritual journey is success.)

WORSHIP: SURRENDERING YOUR LIFE TO HONOR GOD

42. I consistently participate in Sunday and midweek worship experiences at church.

1	2	3	4	5
POOR				OUTSTANDING

43. My heart breaks over the things that break God's heart.

1	2	3	4	5
POOR				OUTSTANDING

44. I regularly give thanks to God.

1	2	3	4	5
POOR				OUTSTANDING

45. I'm living a life that, overall, honors God.

1	2	3	4	5
POOR				OUTSTANDING

46. I have an attitude of wonder and awe toward God.

1	2	3	4	5
POOR				OUTSTANDING

47. I often use the free access I have into God's presence.

1	2	3	4	5
POOR				OUTSTANDING

TOTAL:_____

Take time to answer the following questions to further evaluate your spiritual health. You can do this after your small group meets if you don't have time during the meeting. If you need help with this, schedule a time with your small group leader to talk about your spiritual health.

48. Make a list of your top five priorities. You can get a good idea of your priorities by evaluating how you spend your time. Be realistic and honest. Are your priorities are in the right order? Do you need to get rid of some or add new priorities? (As a student you may have some limitations. This isn't ammo for dropping out of school or disobeying parents!)

49. List 10 things you're thankful for.

50. What influences, directs, guides, or controls you the most?

DAILY BIBLE READINGS

As you meet with your small group for Bible study, prayer, and encouragement, you'll grow spiritually. But no matter how wonderful your small group experience, you need to learn to grow spiritually on your own, too. God has given you an incredible tool to help—his love letter, the Bible. The Bible reveals God's love for you and gives directions for living life to the fullest.

To help you with this, we've included a fairly easy way to read through one of the Gospels. Instead of feeling like you need to sit down and read the entire book at once, we've broken down the reading into bite-size chunks. Check off the passages as you read them. Don't feel guilty if you miss a daily reading. Simply do your best to develop the habit of being in God's Word daily.

A 30-Day Journey Through the Gospel of Matthew

Imagine sitting at the feet of Jesus himself: the Teacher who knows how to live life well, the Savior who died for you, the Lord who commands the universe. Like his first disciples, you can follow him around, watch what he does, listen to what he says, and pattern your life after his.

Day 1	Matthew 1–2
Day 2	Matthew 3
Day 3	Matthew 4
Day 4	Matthew 5:1–20
Day 5	Matthew 5:21–48
Day 6	Matthew 6
Day 7	Matthew 7
Day 8	Matthew 8
Day 9	Matthew 9
Day 10	Matthew 10
Day 11	Matthew 11
Day 12	Matthew 12:1–21
Day 13	Matthew 12:22–50

HOW TO STUDY THE BIBLE ON YOUR OWN

The Bible is the foundation for all the books in the EXPERIENCING CHRIST TOGETHER series. Every lesson contains a Bible passage for your small group to study and apply. To maximize the impact of your small group experience, it's helpful if each participant spends time reading and studying the Bible during the week. When you read the Bible for yourself, you can have discussions based on what *you* know the Bible says instead of what another member has heard second- or third-hand about the Bible.

Growing Christians learn to study the Bible so they can grow spiritually on their own. Here are some principles about studying the Bible to help you give God's Word a central place in your life.

Choose a Time and Place

Since we are easily distracted, pick a time when you're at your best. If you're a morning person, then study the Bible in the morning. Find a place away from phones, computers, and TVs so you are less likely to be interrupted.

Begin with Prayer

Acknowledge God's presence with you. Thank him for his gifts, confess your sins, and ask for his guidance and understanding as you study his love letter to you.

Start with Excitement

We often take God's Word for granted and forget what an incredible gift we have. God wasn't forced to reach out to us, but he did. He's made it possible for us to know him, understand his directions, and be encouraged—all through his Word, the Bible. Remind yourself how amazing it is that God wants you to know him.

Read the Passage

After choosing a passage, read it several times. You might want to read it slowly, pausing after each sentence. If possible, read it out loud. (Remember that before the Bible was written on paper, it was spoken verbally from generation to generation.)

Keep a Journal

Respond to God's Word by writing down how you're challenged, truths to remember, thanksgiving and praise, sins to confess, commands to obey, or any other thoughts you have.

Dig Deep

When you read the Bible, look deeper than the plain meaning of the words. Here are a few ideas about what to look for:

- *Truth about God's character.* What do the verses reveal about God's character?

- *Truth about your life and our world.* You don't have to figure out life on your own. Life can be difficult, but when you know how the world works, you can make good decisions guided by wisdom from God.

- *Truth about the world's past.* The Bible reveals God's intervention in our mistakes and triumphs throughout history. The choices we read about—good and bad—serve as examples to challenge us to greater faith and obedience. (See Hebrews 11:1-12:1.)

- *Truth about our actions.* God will never leave you stranded. Although he allows us all to go through hard times, he is always with us. Our actions have consequences and rewards. Just like he does in Bible stories, God can use all of the consequences and rewards caused by our actions to help others.

As you read, ask these four questions to help you learn from the Bible:

- What do these verses teach me about who God is, how he acts, and how people respond?

- What does this passage teach about the nature of the world?

- What wisdom can I learn from what I read?

- How should I change my life because of what I learned from these verses?

Ask Questions

You may be tempted to skip over parts you don't understand, but don't give up too easily. Understanding the Bible can be hard work. If you come across a word you don't know, look it up in a regular dictionary or a Bible dictionary. If you come across a verse that seems to contradict another verse, see whether your Bible has any notes to explain it. Write down your questions and ask someone who has more knowledge about the Bible than you. Buy or borrow a study Bible or check the Internet. Try *www.gotquestions.org* or *www.carm.org* for answers to your questions.

Apply the Truth to Your Life

The Bible should make a difference in your life. It contains the help you need to live the life God intended. Knowledge of the Bible without personal obedience is worthless and causes hypocrisy and pride. Take time to consider the condition of your thinking, attitudes, and actions, and wonder about how God is working in you. Think about your life situation and how you can serve others better.

More Helpful Ideas

- Decide that the time you have set aside for Bible reading and study is nonnegotiable. Don't let other activities squeeze Bible study time out of your schedule.

- Avoid the extremes of being ritualistic (reading a chapter just to mark it off a list) and being lazy (giving up).

- Begin with realistic goals and boundaries for your study time. If five to seven minutes a day proves a challenge at the beginning, make it a goal to start smaller and increase your time slowly. Don't set yourself up to fail.

- Be open to the leading and teaching of God's Spirit.

- Love God like he's the best friend you'll ever have—which is the truth!

MEMORY VERSES

The word *memory* may cause some of you to groan. In school, you have to memorize dates, places, times, and outcomes. Now you have to memorize the Bible?

No, not the entire Bible! Start small with some key verses. Trust us, this is important. Here's why: Scripture memorization is a good habit for a growing Christian to develop because when God's Word is planted in your mind and heart, it has a way of influencing how you live. King David understood this: "I have hidden your word in my heart that I might not sin against you" (Psalm 119:11).

Challenge one another in your small group to memorize the six verses below—one for each time your small group meets. Hold each other accountable by asking about one another's progress. Write the verses on index cards and keep them handy so you can learn and review them when you have a free moment (standing in line, before class starts, sitting at a red light, when you've finished a test and others are still working, waiting for your dad to get out of the bathroom—you get the picture). You'll be surprised at how many verses you can memorize as you work toward this goal and add verses to your list.

"IN YOUR ANGER DO NOT SIN; WHEN YOU ARE ON YOUR BEDS, SEARCH YOUR HEARTS AND BE SILENT." —PSALM 4:4

"I KNEW THAT YOU ARE A GRACIOUS AND COMPASSIONATE GOD, SLOW TO ANGER AND ABOUNDING IN LOVE, A GOD WHO RELENTS FROM SENDING CALAMITY." —JONAH 4:2

"HE WHO SPEAKS ON HIS OWN DOES SO TO GAIN HONOR FOR HIM-SELF, BUT HE WHO WORKS FOR THE HONOR OF THE ONE WHO SENT HIM IS A MAN OF TRUTH; THERE IS NOTHING FALSE ABOUT HIM." —JOHN 7:18

"IN HIS GRACE, GOD HAS GIVEN US DIFFERENT GIFTS FOR DOING CERTAIN THINGS WELL." —ROMANS 12:6A NLT

"WORK WILLINGLY AT WHATEVER YOU DO, AS THOUGH YOU WERE WORKING FOR THE LORD RATHER THAN FOR PEOPLE."
—COLOSSIANS 3:23 NLT

"EACH ONE SHOULD TEST HIS OWN ACTIONS. THEN HE CAN TAKE PRIDE IN HIMSELF, WITHOUT COMPARING HIMSELF TO SOMEBODY ELSE." —GALATIANS 6:4

JOURNALING: SNAPSHOTS OF YOUR HEART

In the simplest terms, journaling is reflection with pen in hand. A growing life needs time to reflect, so several times throughout this book you're asked to journal. In addition, you always have a journaling option at the end of each session. Through these writing opportunities, you're getting a taste of what it means to journal.

When you take time to write your thoughts in a journal, you'll experience many benefits. A journal is more than a diary—it's a series of snapshots of your heart. The goal of journaling is to slow down your life to capture some of the great, crazy, wonderful, chaotic, painful, encouraging, angering, confusing, joyful, and loving thoughts, feelings, and ideas in your life. Keeping a journal can become a powerful habit when you reflect on your life and how God is working in it.

Personal Insights

When confusion abounds in your life, disorderly thoughts and feelings often loom just out of range, slightly out of focus. Putting these thoughts and feelings on paper is like corralling and domesticating wild beasts. Once on paper, you can look at them, consider them, contemplate the reasons they were causing you pain, and learn from them.

Have you ever had trouble answering the question, "How do you feel?" Journaling compels you to become more specific with your generalized thoughts and feelings. This is not to suggest that a page full of words perfectly represents what's happening on the inside. That would be foolish. But journaling can move you closer to understanding more about yourself.

Reflection and Examination

With journaling, you can write about your feelings, your situations, how you responded to events. You can reflect and answer questions like these:

- Was that the right response?

- What were my other options?

- Did I lose control and act impulsively?

- If this happened again, should I do the same thing? Would I do the same thing?

- How can I be different as a result of this situation?

Spiritual Insights

One of the main goals of journaling is to gain new spiritual insights about God, yourself, and the world. When you take time to journal, you have the opportunity to pause and consider how God is working in your life and in the lives of those around you. Journaling helps you see the work he's accomplishing and remember it for the future.

What to Write About

There isn't one right way to journal, no set number of times per week, no rules for the length of each journal entry. Figure out what works best for you. Get started with these options:

Write a letter or prayer to God

Many Christians struggle with maintaining a consistent prayer life. Writing out your prayers can help strengthen it. Begin with this question: "What do I want to tell God right now?"

Write a letter or conversation to another person

Sometimes conversations with others can be difficult because we're not sure what we ought to say. Have you ever walked away from an interaction and 20 minutes later thought, *I should have said...*? Journaling conversations before they happen can help you think through the issues and approach your interactions with others in intentional ways. As a result, you can feel confident as you begin your conversations because you've taken time to consider the issues beforehand.

Process conflict and pain

You may find it helpful to write about your conflicts with others, especially those that take you by surprise. By journaling soon after conflict occurs, you can reflect and learn from it. You'll be better prepared for the next time you face a similar situation. Conflicts are generally difficult to navigate. Thinking through and writing about specific conflicts typically yields helpful personal insights.

When you're experiencing pain is also a good time to settle your thoughts and consider the nature of your feelings. The great thing about exploring your feelings is that you're only accountable to God. You don't have to worry about hurting anyone's feelings by what you write in your journal (if you keep it private).

Examine your motives

The Bible is clear regarding two heart truths. First, how you behave reflects who you are on the inside (Luke 6:45). Second, you can take the right action for the wrong reason (James 4:3).

The condition of your heart is vitally important. Molding your motives to God's desires is central to following Christ. The Pharisees did many of the right things, but for the wrong reasons. Reflect on the *real* reasons why you do what you do.

Anticipate your actions

Have you ever gone to bed thinking, *That was a mistake. I didn't intend that to happen!* Probably! No one is perfect. You can't predict all of the consequences of your actions. But reflecting on how your actions could affect others will guide you and help you relate better to others.

Reflect on God's work in your life

If you journal in the evening, you can answer this question: "What did God teach me today?"

If you journal in the morning, you can answer this question: "God, what were you trying to teach me yesterday that I missed?" When you reflect on yesterday's events, you may find a common theme that God may have been weaving into your life during the day—one you missed because you were busy. When you see God's hand in your life, even a day later, you know God loves you and is guiding you.

Record insights from Scripture

Journal about whatever you learn from the Bible. Rewrite a verse in your own words or figure out how a passage is structured. Try to uncover the key truths from the verses and see how the verses apply to your life. (Again, there is no right way to journal. The only wrong way is to not try it at all.)

JOURNAL PAGES

JOURNAL PAGES

JOURNAL PAGES

JOURNAL PAGES

JOURNAL PAGES

JOURNAL PAGES

PRAYING IN YOUR SMALL GROUP

As believers, we're called to support each other in prayer, and prayer should be a consistent part of a healthy small group.

One of prayer's purposes is aligning our hearts with God's. By doing this, we can more easily get in touch with what's at the center of God's heart. Prayer shouldn't be a how-well-did-I-do performance or a self-conscious, put-on-the-spot task to fear. Your small group may need time to get comfortable with praying out loud, too. That's okay.

When you do pray, silently or aloud, follow the practical, simple words of Jesus in Matthew 6:

Pray sincerely.

"And when you pray, do not be like the hypocrites, for they love to pray standing in the synagogues and on the street corners to be seen by men. I tell you the truth, they have received their reward in full." (Matthew 6:5)

In the Old Testament, God's people were disciplined prayer warriors. They developed specific prayers to use for every special occasion or need. They had prayers for light and darkness, prayers for fire and rain, prayers for good news and bad. They even had prayers for travel, holidays, holy days, and Sabbath days.

Every day the faithful would stop to pray at 9 a.m., noon, and 3 p.m.—a sort of religious coffee break. Their ritual was impressive, to say the least, but being legalistic had its downside. The proud, self-righteous types would strategically plan their schedules to be in the middle of a crowd when it was time for prayer so everyone could hear them as they prayed loudly. You can see the problem. What was intended to promote spiritual passion became a drama to impress others.

God wants our prayers addressed to him alone. That seems obvious enough, yet how many of us pray wanting to impress our listeners rather than wanting to truly communicate with God? This is the problem if you're prideful like the Pharisees about the excellent quality of your prayers. But it can also be a problem if you're new to prayer and are concerned that you don't know how to "pray right." Don't concern yourself with what others think; just talk to God as if you were sitting in a chair next to him.

Pray simply.

"And when you pray, do not keep on babbling like pagans, for they think they will be heard because of their many words. Do not be like them, for your Father knows what you need before you ask him." (Matthew 6:7-8)

God isn't looking to be dazzled with brilliantly crafted language. Nor is he impressed with lengthy monologues. It's freeing to know that he wants us to keep it simple.

Pray specifically.

"This, then, is how you should pray: 'Our Father in heaven, hallowed be your name, your kingdom come, your will be done on earth as it is in heaven. Give us today our daily bread. Forgive us our debts, as we also have forgiven our debtors. And lead us not into temptation, but deliver us from the evil one." (Matthew 6:9-13)

What the church has come to call "The Lord's Prayer" is a model of the kind of brief but specific prayers we may offer anytime, anywhere. Look at some of the specific items mentioned:

- Adoration: "hallowed be your name"

- Provision: "your kingdom come...your will be done...give us today our daily bread"

- Forgiveness: "forgive us our debts"

- Protection: "lead us not into temptation"

PRAYER REQUEST GUIDELINES

Because prayer time is so vital, group members need some basic guidelines for sharing, handling, and praying for prayer requests. Without a commitment from each person to honor these simple suggestions, prayer time can become dominated by one person, an opportunity to gossip, or a never-ending story time. (There are appropriate times to tell personal stories, but this may not be the best time.)

Here are a few suggestions for each group to consider:

Write down prayer requests.

Each small group member should write down every prayer request on the "Prayer Request" pages provided. When you commit to a small group, you're agreeing to be part of the spiritual community, and that includes praying for one another. By keeping track of prayer requests, you can see how God answers them. You'll be amazed at God's power and faithfulness.

As an alternative, one person can record the requests and e-mail them to the rest of the group. If your group chooses this option, safeguard confidentiality. Be sure personal information isn't compromised. Some people share e-mail accounts with parents or siblings. Develop a workable plan for this option.

Give everybody an opportunity to share.

As a group, consider the amount of time remaining and the number of people who still want to share. You won't be able to share every thought or detail about a situation.

Obviously if someone experiences a crisis, you may need to focus exclusively on that group member by giving him or her extended time and focused prayer. (However, true crises are infrequent.)

The leader can limit the time by making a comment such as one of the following:

- We have time for everyone to share one praise or request.

- Simply share what to pray for. We can talk in more detail later.

- We're only going to pray for requests about the people in our group. How can we pray for you specifically?

- We've run out of time to share prayer requests. Take a moment to write down your prayer request and give it to me [or identify another person]. You'll get them by e-mail tomorrow.

Just as people are free to share, they're free to not share.

The goal of a healthy small group should be to create an environment where participants feel comfortable sharing about their lives. Still, not everyone needs to share each week. Here's what I tell my small group:

> *As a small group we're here to support one another in prayer. This doesn't mean that everyone has to share something. In fact, don't assume you have to share at all. There's no need to make up prayer requests just to have something to say. If you have something you'd like the group to pray for, let us know. If not, that's fine, too.*

No gossip allowed.

Don't allow sharing prayer requests to become an excuse for gossip. If you're not part of the problem or solution, consider the information gossip. Share the request without the story behind it—that helps prevent gossip. Also speak in general terms without giving names or details ("I have a friend who's in trouble. God knows who it is. Pray for me that I can be a good friend.").

If a prayer request starts going astray, someone should kindly intercede, perhaps with a question such as, "How can we pray for you in this situation?"

Don't give advice or try to fix the problem.

When people share their struggles and problems, a common response is to try to fix the problem by offering advice. At the right time, the group might provide input on a particular problem, but during prayer time, keep focused on praying for the need. Often God's best work in a person's life comes through times of struggle and pain.

Keep in touch.

Make sure you exchange phone numbers and e-mail addresses before you leave the first meeting. That way you can contact someone who needs prayer or encouragement before the next time your group meets. You can write each person's contact information on the "Small Group Roster" (page 97).

PRAYER OPTIONS

There's no single, correct way to end all your sessions. In addition to the options provided in each session, here are some additional ideas.

During the Small Group Gathering

- One person closes in prayer for the entire group.

- Pray silently. Have one person close the silent prayer time after a while with "amen."

- The leader or another group member prays out loud for each person in the group.

- Everyone prays for one request or person. This can be done randomly during prayer or, as the request is shared, a willing person can announce, "I'll pray for that."

- Everyone who wants to pray takes a turn. Not everyone needs to pray out loud.

- Split the group in half and pray together in smaller groups.

- Pair up and pray for each other.

- On occasion, each person can share what he or she is thankful for before a prayer request, so prayer requests don't become negative from focusing only on problems. Prayer isn't just asking for stuff—it also includes praising God and being thankful for his generosity toward us.

- If you're having an animated discussion about a Bible passage or a life situation, don't feel like you must cut it short for prayer requests. Use it as an opportunity to add a little variety to the prayer time by praying some other day between sessions.

Outside the Group Time

You can use these options if you run out of time to pray during the meeting or in addition to prayer during the meeting.

- Send prayer requests to each other via e-mail.

- Pick prayer partners and phone each other during the week.

- Have each person in the small group choose a day to pray for everyone in the group. Perhaps you can work it out to have each day of the week covered. Let participants report back at each meeting for accountability.

- Have each person pray for just one other person in the group for the entire week. (Everyone prays for the person on the left or on the right or draw names.)

PRAYER REQUEST LOG

DATE	NAME	REQUEST	ANSWER

PRAYER REQUEST LOG

DATE	NAME	REQUEST	ANSWER

PRAYER REQUEST LOG

DATE

NAME

REQUEST

ANSWER

PRAYER REQUEST LOG

DATE	NAME	REQUEST	ANSWER

PRAYER REQUEST LOG

DATE	NAME	REQUEST	ANSWER

PRAYER REQUEST LOG

DATE	NAME	REQUEST	ANSWER

EXPERIENCING CHRIST TOGETHER FOR A YEAR

Your group will benefit the most if you work through the entire EXPE-RIENCING CHRIST TOGETHER series. The longer your group is to-gether, the better your chances of maturing spiritually and integrating the biblical purposes into your life. Here's a plan to complete the series in one year.

Begin with a planning meeting and review the books in the series. They are:

Book 1—Beginning in Jesus: Six Sessions on the Life of Christ

Book 2—Connecting in Jesus: Six Sessions on Fellowship

Book 3—Growing in Jesus: Six Sessions on Discipleship

Book 4—Serving Like Jesus: Six Sessions on Ministry

Book 5—Sharing Jesus: Six Sessions on Evangelism

Book 6—Surrendering to Jesus: Six Sessions on Worship

We recommend you begin with *Book 1—Beginning in Jesus: Six Sessions on the Life of Christ,* because it contains an introduction to six qualities of Jesus. After that, you can use the books in any order that works for your particular ministry.

As you look at your youth ministry calendar, you may want to tailor the order in which you study the books to complement events your youth group will experience. For example, if you plan to have an evangelism out-reach, study *Book 5—Sharing Jesus: Six Sessions on Evangelism* first to build momentum. Or study *Book 4—Serving Like Jesus: Six Sessions on Ministry* in late winter to prepare for the spring break missions trip.

Use your imagination and celebrate the completion of each book. Have a worship service, an outreach party, a service project, a fun night out, a meet-the-family dinner, or whatever else you can dream up.

Number of Weeks	Meeting Topic
1	Planning meeting—a casual gathering to get acquainted, discuss expectations, and refine the covenant (page 18).
6	Beginning in Jesus: Six Sessions on the Life of Christ
1	Celebration
6	Connecting in Jesus: Six Sessions on Fellowship
1	Celebration
6	Growing in Jesus: Six Sessions on Discipleship
1	Celebration
6	Serving Like Jesus: Six Sessions on Ministry
1	Celebration
6	Sharing Jesus: Six Sessions on Evangelism
1	Celebration
6	Surrendering to Jesus: Six Sessions on Worship
1	Celebration
2	Christmas Break
1	Easter Break
6	Summer Break

ABOUT THE AUTHORS

A youth ministry veteran of 25 years, **Doug Fields** has authored or co-authored more than 40 books, including *Purpose-Driven® Youth Ministry* and *Your First Two Years in Youth Ministry*. With an M.Div. from Fuller Theological Seminary, Doug is a teaching pastor and pastor to students at Saddleback Church in Southern California and president of Simply Youth Ministry. He and his wife, Cathy, have three children.

Brett Eastman has served as the leader of small groups for both Willow Creek Community Church and Saddleback Church. Brett is now the founder and CEO of LIFETOGETHER, a ministry whose mission is to "transform lives through community." Brett earned his masters of divinity degree from Talbot School of Theology and lives in Southern California.